It's NOT Just a Game

How Parents and Gamers Can Apply God's Word to Video Games

Carl Kerby Jr.
Drew Thorwall

It's NOT Just a Game:
How Parents and Gamers Can Apply God's Word to Video Games

© 2013 by Carl Kerby Jr. and Drew Thorwall
Edited by Sean Thorwall

ISBN: 978-0-9915509-0-6

Printed in the United States of America.

Cover art illustration by Jesse Pie

Special Thanks

To Tish Kerby and Melissa Thorwall, for their encouragement during this time-consuming process, and for believing us when we said we were playing games for research.

For our children, Trey and Naomi Kerby and Belle, Axel, Obed, and Simeon Thorwall. We pray that what we have learned here will bless them as they grow.

To our parents, Carl and Masami Kerby and Brent and Vicki Thorwall, for letting us play games when our homework was done, and giving us the skills to play with discernment.

Table of Contents

Note from the Authors

SPOILER ALERT! This book will "spoil" the endings to many of the video games discussed, because the ending is often when the game drives its message home. The goal in this book is to reveal the spiritual messages that are present in video games regarding Christianity and to equip you to answer each challenge from the Bible.

This book will not tell you which games to play or not play. It will not tell you which games to let your children play, or not play. Instead, it will show you how to challenge the gamer in your house—whether that is you or your child—to think critically when gaming, equipping you to answer the challenges in games as you encounter them together.

Drew Thorwall
Carl Kerby Jr.

Foreword

PUT YOUR STEEL toed boots on, my friends. If you think that "It's just a game!" and you don't need to be concerned with the messages that are being portrayed in this medium, you are along for a bumpy ride! In fact, you may want to put your seat belt on as well.

I'll never forget when my son, Carl Kerby Jr. came to me and said, "Dad, I've got an idea for your next book. You've got to write about video games! You can use it as a follow up to your book on TV and media." Yeah right! The only video games that I even attempt to play are Dr. Mario and Mario Kart. ("I'ma Wario, I'ma gonna' win!!") Needless to say my response wasn't that positive. To be honest, I blew him off.

He was persistent though. I told him that I couldn't write about video games because I don't know about video games. I've always believed that you can only talk about what you know about. I don't like speaking on topics with which I'm not familiar. People know very quickly when you're blowing smoke at them and they'll come after you when they see you faking it.

So, my son said, "I'll write it and give it to you. You just tweak it and put your name on it!" Thus started, "the book!" Carl Jr. started doing research and bringing me pieces to use in my talks. To be honest, I was shocked. I'd played "computer games" starting back with Pong on Atari! When the Commodore 64 came out I was in the military and thought I was the man. I had over 1,000 games. Truth be told, they were all lame, but I had a box of floppy discs and was king of the hill. But what my son was showing me was NOTHING like I had ever seen in video games. Something had changed and I had missed it!

When he finally pulled together enough to start a book he brought it to me and said to rework it and put my name on it. Of course, I couldn't do it! It wasn't my work. So it sat for over a year. That's when the Lord opened the door for me to bring him on staff at Reasons for Hope. Shortly after that I told him, "You've got your first book, and by the way you're giving your first talk on gaming in 3 days!"

I knew Carl Jr. was onto something when we visited a church where he asked if any of them allowed their children to watch "R" rated movies. That sparked my attention. No one raised their hand. He then asked if anyone allowed their children to play, *Assassin's Creed, Call of Duty, Bioshock, Call of Juarez* etc. Hands went up all over the room. His response hooked me:

"Parents, do you realize that you won't let your child watch an "R" rated movie, but you'll allow them to play an "R" rated game?"

Ouch! He then explained how TV shows and movies are relatively short compared to videogames in which children invest 25, 50, even 100 plus hours. And they are most definitely not passive! You name a character after yourself then choose what to do and to whom you want to do it!

Parents opened up and started asking questions. Since that time I've watched repeatedly as parents have been shown things they didn't have a clue about. Recently I spoke after Carl Jr. and asked the parents if they thought the information they had received was important. I wanted them to speak with me in between sessions. I was shocked by the response. Hands went up all over the room; they wanted to give me feedback right then. Overwhelmingly they told me "Thank you! We had no idea. We can now have a conversation with our children over this topic!" Mission Accomplished!!

Maybe you're saying to yourself, "We don't let our children

play games!" Praise God! But guess what, they will leave the home someday and get exposed to them. They do have friends that play them and by preparing them to critically evaluate the messages that are in there you are preparing them to minister to their peers. AND, most importantly, this will allow you to explain to your children WHY you made that choice in the first place.

I've always believed that rules with out reasons, lead to rebellion. Read the book and watch the video resources that Carl Jr. and Drew have put together. Get answers for the challenges in games, then start the conversation!

Carl Kerby Sr.

Introduction

WHAT ROLE DO video games play in the life of a follower of Christ, if any? Are they an escape? An addiction? An art form? Are they evil, or can they be honoring to God? Why write a book about Christianity in video games at all? Our answer to that last question is: to equip you to answer the challenges to the Bible that are present in some games.

Carl and I have been gamers for virtually our entire lives. Being born the year before Nintendo released its first home console to the U.S. can have that effect on a boy. We have had many debates over the best games, best systems, best levels, and more. We have some of the rarest pieces of gaming history in our collections. Suffice to say, we know the gaming culture inside and out because we're part of it! We're excited because we now realize that there are many spiritual conversations to be had with gamers based on their own games!

It may surprise you that the focus in this book is not the issues that most often drive video games into the public debate. Video games have become a comfortable undercurrent, steadily growing in our technological and media savvy lives. Often overlooked as benign additions to our gadgets and living rooms, the nature of the medium can passively shape the worldviews of players who absorb the content they deliver. Even games rated "E for Everyone" may be deemed safe by families, unaware of the spiritual warfare going on within the programming code. As gamers and parents, we latch on to the all-too-familiar refrain "it's just a game!"

It's not just a game! Video games function uniquely among other media formats. While most media are passive (sit and

1

watch, sit and listen, sit and read), video games are interactive. The player is an essential part of ensuring that the content, and thus the message, are delivered. The player's involvement in "achieving" the message by furthering the story, beating the game, or even playing at all can lead to subtle absorption of the "truth" as presented by the game.

In his provocative book *Technopoly*, Neil Postman explains that "once a [new] technology is admitted, it plays out its hand; it does what it is designed to do. Our task is to understand what that design is—that is to say, when we admit a new technology to the culture, we must do so with our eyes wide open."[1] Though the medium itself may inherently be neither good nor evil, there is no doubt that its intrinsic qualities shape the messages, how they are delivered, and how they are received.

Take, for instance, a game in which the player is given the chance to either partner with God or turn against Him (a surprisingly prolific scenario). This is the point the player has spent hours honing a skill to reach, to achieve, to earn! You've reached the end of the game, only to find out that the best ending only comes by denying or defeating God! It all goes up in smoke if they don't take the initiative to press the button on the controller that corresponds with a denial of God.

As a gamer myself, I know that in these moments you are much more focused on the emotion of the story, the adrenaline of accomplishment, and any number of other factors, than you are on carefully critiquing the truth or error of the character's actions. Spiritual senses can be slowed because your current focus is on advancing, achieving, and beating the game! Likewise, in games where various temptations are presented to the in-game character's choice, a gamer may feel the freedom to give in to those temptations because "it's just a game." This choice feels disconnected from reality and consequence, even

---

1. Postman, Neil, *Technopoly: The Surrender of Culture to Technology* (New York: Vintage, 1993), 7.

as it has a very real spiritual impact on the heart.

These secular messages are at times unintentional, a sad byproduct of a secular society, rather than an open attack. Even so, they are present and worth discussing. At other times, secular messages are included to explore a theme, such as the value or danger of organized religion. Still other times, the secular messages are absolutely overt and amount to no less than an intentional attack on the truth of Scripture.

Regardless of why the secular messages are delivered, they present an important opportunity to think critically. This is why gamers must know God's Word, ask tough questions, and not let the game teach them, but challenge any statements in the game. We must keep our eyes wide open!

1 Thessalonians 5:21 says "Test everything. Hold on to the good." That is the challenge undertaken in this book. It does not set out to destroy the credibility or playability of games. We, the authors, are gamers and enjoy the time spent on this creative, artistic pastime! We have found a simple strategy to engage culture with the Bible is to "Know it. Live it. Share it."

The goal is to know God's Word first, and how to use it as a filter for truth when we play video games. Then we can live it out: not writing off what we interact with in the game, but testing everything and holding on to the good. We can use those very games as an open door to spiritual conversations and opportunities to share the gospel of Jesus with gamers.

Know it. Live it. Share it.
Drew Thorwall

1

Once Upon a Game

It's NOT Just a Game

"IT'S JUST A game." Have you heard this claim before? Maybe even spoken it yourself? It is the number one response we get from gamers and parents whenever we talk about the dangers of unbiblical messages in games. Gamers may be tempted to write-off the discussion in this book by repeating that familiar phrase. We know, because we are gamers and we are parents. We can feel defensive about our favorite games, responding that the developers didn't intentionally bash Christianity. "It was just for story!" or "That's the bad guy, it's not like they're telling me to do it!"

There's an element of truth here, but also a much bigger picture. Think about it this way: You are a parent and you hire a babysitter to watch the children while you and your spouse enjoy a night out. Now let's say the babysitter turns out to be an atheist. Well, it's just a babysitter right? But what if you find out that every time you're out, the babysitter is telling the children why it's silly to believe in God, or that He isn't real. Even though you can try to correct the children's thinking, they are hearing this message repeatedly from a source they spend a lot of time with.

What do you do? Do you continue to employ that particular babysitter even though you know they might lead your children to a life apart from God? Of course not! You would never say "it's just a babysitter," and you should never say "it's just a game" either!

The truth is: games have messages. They may be subtle or overt, intentional or unintentional, but you as a gamer, or perhaps your children, spend a lot of time with games that may be telling them dangerous things. As followers of Christ, we need to get smart about gaming.

It is also worth noting that one bad babysitter doesn't spoil the bunch. It would be pointless to go into anti-babysitter mode and never hire a babysitter again. Instead, you would be careful to interview each babysitter to make sure they were safe for your children. The same goes for games. This book will not tell you to throw them all out and it won't necessarily tell you which ones to specifically avoid either. Our goal is to equip you to apply the Bible and do the critical thinking yourself, no matter what game you face, even if it's not covered here!

Game creators know it's NOT just a game anymore. You will see in our discussion of *The Binding of Isaac*, for example, a game developer who specifically states that he created his game as a commentary on his own negative religious experience. He goes so far as to state that gamers may miss his intention, but that it was nonetheless the driving force behind the game![1]

Similarly, in February of 2013, a report came out that a developer of the game *Bioshock Infinite*[2] resigned his position over the spiritual content in the closing moments in this game.[3] It was only after the game's creator, Ken Levine, had a long conversation and agreed to change some of the content that the developer decided to stick around. In that article, Levine com-

---

1.   See Chapter 4
2.   Sequel to *Bioshock*, also discussed in Chapter 4
3.   http://www.gamespot.com/news/Bioshock-infinites-religious-themes-led-dev-to-consider-quitting-6404620

mented, "I realized that something I could connect to was a notion of forgiveness and what an important part that is of the New Testament and why Christ was such a revolutionary figure."

What is the point of those two stories? Both situations demonstrate how the game creators themselves believe that it is not just a game! They make bold statements that the purpose of their games is to explore religious themes and spirituality, not just for plot. They even consider it important enough to quit very lucrative jobs in the gaming industry over the very real spiritual warfare in the programming code. Games are full of spiritual topics just begging to be explored!

Even when it is difficult to know exactly what developers intended regarding spiritual things, there is no doubt when it is contrary to Scripture. Regardless of intent, the content is worth testing to make sure that we are grounded in God's Word, not buying into the stereotypes of a culture that wants us to get comfortable with attacks against God's Word.

Growing Up Gaming

Would you be surprised to learn that 59% of the U.S. population play video games? Odds are, you're one of them! We are too, as well as many of the children, young adults, young parents, and families today. The vast majority of children play video games, yet make up only 32% of the gaming population, meaning there are also a lot of adults. According to the Entertainment Software Association, the other 68% are over the age of 18, with the average age of gamers being in their thirties!

What was once considered a pastime for children and boys now permeates every demographic. In fact, adult women are a greater percentage of the gaming population (30%) than the stereotypical boy of 17 and under (18%).[4] Games have become culture. Games have become identity as more of the population

---

4.   www.theesa.com/facts/gameplayer.asp

can't remember a time that they were not gamers.

What about you? What is your earliest memory? Do you remember the first house where you grew up? Do you remember your first pet? Or the songs your mother used to sing to you in your bed? One of Carl's earliest memories is directly tied to his introduction to video games.

When Carl was four years old, his parents would drop him off at a local daycare while they went to work. This was a nice daycare with a playground and all the books and toys a normal child would want. However, none of these things caught Carl's interest. While all the other children were having fun playing together, there was only one thing that grabbed his attention. A Nintendo Entertainment System (NES) nestled in the corner of the room.

The first time he grabbed that grey controller, Carl was hooked. He would play *Super Mario Bros.* every day, learning every secret in order to master the game. He seemed to have a natural skill at playing video games and was happily sucked into a world of Goombas, Koopa Troopas and Piranha Plants.

Each day when his mom picked him up from day-care, she would ask Carl how his day was. He told her all about his best friend, Mario, and their adventures together. Over time, his stories would get more and more detailed. Carl's mom kept wondering, "Who is this Mario person? It's good to see little Carl making some friends!" It wasn't until much later that she realized that his "friend" was just a character in the game! This was Carl's first foray into a life of video gaming.

Growing up, Carl couldn't see how games could have any negative effects. His parents even found ways to use the NES as a positive motivator for him. Somewhat surprisingly, 63% of all parents believe that video games are a positive part of their children's lives.[5] For example, Carl's parents would say, "You can't play Nintendo until you finish your homework!" He would

---

5.   www.usernetsite.com/society/new-video-game-statistics.php

run to his backpack and complete every school assignment as quickly, if not thoroughly, as possible just for the opportunity to play the next game.

Gaming even became a family affair. Carl's father enjoyed gaming as well, and although he was not hooked quite like Carl was, they would sit down and play video games together. The family's first gaming system was the Commodore 64.

Carl remembers that the game quality was terrible back then, but that didn't bother him. He still wanted to play any time he had the chance. His dad would invite the basketball team to the house after every practice to play video games. Friends had a blast playing games like *Mario Kart* on the Nintendo 64. They still hook up that game system to this day when friends come over to hang out. His father tried to recommend video games that were family friendly. Driving games, puzzle games, and sports games were very common in their house.

At that time, any money given to Carl for Christmas or a birthday would go straight to video games. He read video game magazines and played the "hottest" games out there. Some of the games were rated E (for Everyone) and some were rated M (for Mature). While video games companies are not supposed to sell games rated M to children under the age of 18, Carl was never once questioned about his age. In fact, recent research demonstrates that children successfully purchase M-rated video games 50% of the time. One poll also shows that 50% of young gamers 8-12 years old, and 79% of teens admit to playing M-rated games.[6]

Even as games became a bigger part of Carl's life, he became susceptible to the underlying dangers in some of them. His parents certainly would not have approved of some of the games he played. First person shooters (FPS) were very popular then, as they are now. Carl didn't necessarily enjoy them, but didn't want to be the only one not playing either! So, he

6.   Annual MediaWise – Harris Interactive Poll 2007

grabbed the controller and played along.

One particular FPS led Carl to feelings of guilt for the first time while playing a game. In the game, *TimeSplitters 2*, the player could design their own level, then choose a fighter to have a gun war in the building. Carl and his friends couldn't think of a creative design for a level. His house was too small for creating a fun map. The gym they played basketball at was too wide open. Their school, however, would create the perfect layout. Carl stayed up all night designing a level that looked exactly like his school.

They had a blast playing that level. Having walked the hallways of the school everyday, they knew exactly where all the hiding spots were when playing this virtual recreation. Their characters would walk around and kill each other with whatever weapon they could grab.

One day, Carl's mom walked by his room and saw Carl and his friends playing their school level. Upset with him she said, "You know, it's games like this that make children walk into schools and shoot people," referencing the tragedy at Columbine. Then it hit him. He was playing a video game where he was shooting people in a school building! Carl's heart sank. He felt so much guilt realizing how the interactive nature of the game had subtly drawn him into the process of creating something so negative.

Beyond this eye-opening experience, there was one other game that sharpened Carl's focus on the potential dangers of video gaming. In 2008 one of his all-time favorite games, *Chrono Trigger*, was re-released. What gamers love about this classic most is the dynamic way that the character's in-game decisions have meaningful in-game consequences. There were multiple endings to the game depending on how you played it. Playing it again a second time, however, Carl revisited scenes that he hadn't fully understood when he was just a child.

In one particularly harrowing episode, the Princess has been captured, and it is your challenge to save her. Your travels lead you to an old church, but the congregation is acting a little... mysterious. They say things like:

"We want nothing but world peace... Or a piece of the world, tee,hee..."

"You might like to stick around for the organ recital. It's a real killer!"

"People wouldn't know what to do with themselves in a truly peaceful world! My, what delicious, er ... I mean, delightful looking humans!"

As it turns out, the church members aren't human at all. They are monsters! Your character must defeat them in order to rescue the Princess. In another scene of the game, the group of characters you control enters a town called "Medina Village" where the inhabitants avidly hate humans and worship a being called Magus. Later in the game when you defeat Magus, these villagers completely change. They are friendly and enjoy life.

In retrospect, these scenes demonstrate *Chrono Trigger's* overtly secular worldview, especially about the church. The game presents a church that is full of hypocrites. Characters in the church may have looked nice and friendly, but they were just trying to draw you into church to eat you! On top of that, this part of the game shows a town that is a better place without religion. It is not until you defeat Magus, their "god," that those villagers find true happiness and peace.

Carl's father, who has been in ministry for many years, always taught him that when you discover that something is proclaiming a secular worldview, you need to find out what the Bible has to say on the matter and base your beliefs on a biblical worldview. Carl asked himself a simple question: Is Church a bad thing? The Bible gives us a simple answer.

*"Behold, how good and how pleasant it is for brethren
to dwell together in unity!"* —Psalms 133:1 (NKJV)

*"And over all these virtues put on love, which binds
them all together in perfect unity. Let the peace of
Christ rule in your hearts, since as members of one
body you were called to peace. And be thankful."*
—Colossians 3:14-15

We find answers for the secular worldview in video games
when we go back to the Scripture. But how often do we play
games with a Bible at our side or read the Bible after playing?
Do we even realize that the video games might be teaching us
a secular message? The time has come for us to realize: It's not
just a game!"

When the Ratings Don't Help

Carl's story is a familiar one to many lifelong gamers. While
doing research for this book we tried to understand, "What
changed?" Games used to seem so clean and family friendly.
Why do they look so different today? Is it just our perception, or
has there really been a monumental shift? Being Nintendo fans,
we noticed a significant change from the early 90's to the late
90's. Looking back at the history of the industry, there is one
substantial reason why there has been a drastic change in the
family-friendly nature of video games: the ESRB.

The video game industry is governed in a way that is intended to help parents make informed decisions about the
content in the games they let their children play. The Entertainment Software Rating Board (ESRB) is essential to this purpose. Strangely, the introduction of the rating system in 1994
has opened a floodgate of controversial content in games, including spiritual content.

Before then, there were no rating systems for video games the way there had been in the movie industry. Instead, developers and producers decided what content would be acceptable to the public and what was too controversial. Now, almost anything goes as content can simply be labeled and left to the consumer to decide what comes into their home. It is important for parents to understand the ESRB rating system,[7] as it can be a very helpful tool. Here are just a few examples of the ratings in video games:

EC – Early Childhood
E – Everyone
T – Teen
M – Mature
AO – Adults Only

Prior to the ESRB, Nintendo of America, who dominated the late 80's and early 90's with their Nintendo Entertainment System, Gameboy, and Super Nintendo, stepped up and put very strict policies on what video game content would be allowed in North American homes. Former Nintendo president Hiroshi Yamauchi believed that if the company allowed adult-themed games to be published in the States it would forever tarnish the company's image and give Japan a bad reputation.[8]

According to Nintendo of America's Video Game Content Guidelines, Nintendo would not allow developers to include any material that society deemed as unacceptable. They banned games that had sexually suggestive material, adult language, excessive violence, and games which "reflect ethnic, religious, nationalistic, or sexual stereotypes of language; this includes symbols that are related to any type of racial, religious, nationalistic, or ethnic group, such as crosses, pentagrams, God, Gods (Roman

---

7. For more on individual ratings, visit www.esrb.org for U.S. ratings or www.pegi.info for European ratings.

8. Sheff, David, *Game Over: How Nintendo Conquered the World* (New York: Vintage, 1994).

mythological gods are acceptable), Satan, hell, Buddha."[9]

Today you can hardly turn a corner in a game without finding some use of Christian symbols, songs, or Scripture, but none of that would show up in an ESRB rating! At best it is incidental; at worst it becomes an open attack. In both cases, it needs a response!

Our Focus

This is why our focus is not, as you might have anticipated, on violence, language, drug use, or sexual immorality in games. There are many Christian ministries striving to educate parents and gamers on these issues, and identifying such content is the way in which the ESRB is still a helpful tool.

None of these groups, however, are focused on the unbiblical, secular, and even anti-Christian messages being presented in the video games you will read about in this book. Christians need to be aware of these specific challenges and how to answer them with real truth from the Bible. Our hope is that you are challenged by this book to start those conversations and deal with the challenges head on.

Chapter 2 will provide you a brief overview of the structure of this book so that even if you do not play video games yourself, you will be able to benefit deeply from the discussion of games that follows.

---

9.   www.filibustercartoons.com/Nintendo.php

2

For Parents too!

Parents, take note!

WE HAVE INCLUDED specific examples of games in this book and encourage you to read them, even if you are not a gamer yourself, because these are the games your children play! You need to be proactive in knowing what is out there so that you can start the conversation in your family about what is true and what is an attack against God's Word. You will also see that the specific examples illustrate many of the tough questions people ask about God and the Bible in all areas of life.

As we go through this book, you will gain an understanding of the history of video games (which we refer to as "old-school"), and we will compare those to the video games of today ("new-school"). Parents, you may be used to the old-school games and unaware of the seismic shift in spiritual content that now exists. These games are not just mindless entertainment. They all have worldviews, and they all bear messages.

Many of the games in this book are best-sellers. Odds are high that you or someone you know has played these games. Now the question is: how will you be equipped to answer the challenges to Christ followers found within them? How will you be equipped to start the conversation in your family that leads to a better understanding of God's truth and greater discernment in gaming?

It is critical to master the skill of critical thinking.

> *"But sanctify the Lord God in your hearts: And always be ready to give an answer to everyone who asks you a reason for the hope that is in you, with meekness and fear."* —1 Peter 3:15 (NKJV)

Know it! Live it! Share it!

As Christians, we have an amazing gift in the Bible. We need to "Know it. Live it. Share it." That's one simple way to remember the rhythm of life for a follower of Jesus. We follow Him, learning to live as more mature disciples, and then share the gospel with others!

This book will especially help you know it as we bring Scripture to bear on every challenge presented here. But don't stop there! We want you to take what you know and live it, even in the area of video gaming! That might mean changing which games you play. It might mean taking more responsibility in helping your children make wise gaming choices. It definitely means having more conversations with each other as we play games with our eyes wide open.

Those conversations are where we get the chance to share it. This book provides a lot of starting points for having spiritual conversations with parents, children, and gamers. They don't realize how many spiritual things they absorb every day! Challenge them to think about it! Pray that God shows you the places He is already at work where your conversation can help lead someone else to a deeper understanding of Him. Get equipped to answer these challenges for yourself and share those answers with others.

To help you "Know it! Live it! Share it!" the discussion of each game in this book is organized with a few key components.

Each chapter opens with a look back at the topic's appearance in old-school gaming. It is then followed by discussion of current games in which we address **The Content, The Challenge, The Answers,** and then provide *Conversation Questions* to help parents and gamers get talking!

Chapters are broken down into categories based on the aspect of Christianity the games encounter (i.e. God, the Bible, etc.). These sections include examples of the spiritual and secular worldview content addressed in the game. These are not meant to be exhaustive, but representative. We identify challenges and points for discussion in each example.

Scripture is then used to give answers to those challenges. The overarching goal is not to provide an answer to every situation in every game, but to provide meaningful answers on the common challenges to and attacks on Christianity throughout a variety of popular games and genres. More space will be devoted to games that are particularly important either for their popularity or for their impact on gaming as a place of religious discussion.

Each game discussion is accompanied by *Conversation Questions* to help you get a good grip on how to think through the issues the games raise and share the answers with others.

Parents, use these with your children!

Gamers, use them with your friends!

The discussion in this book provides a great opportunity to have spiritual conversations, not only with Christians, but with seekers who know the world of gaming. We know; we've used it that way already!

Ideally, this book is much more than a reference tool for a specific game, though it can be that. Rather, it is a guide to equip you—the parent, gamer, and Christ-follower—to effectively use the Bible to answer any challenge you may encounter.

Let's look at a brief "case study" to give you a taste of how this book will answer the challenges in games. We will use one of gaming's all-time best-sellers: *Grand Theft Auto 4*.

Case Study: Grand Theft Auto 4

Grand Theft Auto 4 will serve as a case study for how to use this book. *Grand Theft Auto 4* is one of the best-selling games of all time and is no stranger to the media or the attacks of Christians who decry the violence and sexual content therein. The game is filled with prostitutes, drugs, murder, and every combination of them. Those disturbing topics get most of the attention, but the game contains deeper spiritual content that goes unnoticed, and therefore unchallenged, leaving gamers to passively accept it as truth if they are not careful.

First, what is the content of the game? Where does it intersect Christianity? What truth claims does it make? What mistakes or attacks are present?

The Content:

A gang member is talking to the main character, Niko. He says:

> "Jesus? He did some crazy s*** too. I mean, everyone does. He killed people. He killed that John the Baptist cat. He did what He had to."

The Challenge:

Was Jesus a violent killer?

This statement is shocking. The game designers are attempting to provide the player with reasonable cause to commit murders themselves within the context of the game. Not only does it make the statement that Jesus was a murderer, but that He is condoned for it because it was "what He had to do." Did He have to kill John the Baptist? Did He even kill him at all?

Many followers of Christ (or even those who are still questioning God) with a certain level of biblical familiarity could quickly and confidently retort that Jesus was not a murderer. However, not everyone reads the Bible. Not all teens attend church. Not all gamers check facts when playing games. And none of that is a surprise. Would they take this claim as truth? Would they even think to question statements like this? The way the statement is layered even allows for a person to passively accept that Jesus is a murderer, even if they disagree that murder is necessary. There are many paths, but which one presents the truth?

The Answer:

Mark 6 recounts how John the Baptist condemned Herod for marrying Herodias. Herodias was his brother Philip's former wife and his own niece, and she was furious at John the Baptist for speaking the truth about her sinfulness. That is some disturbing stuff and is in violation of Old Testament law. Later, Herodias's daughter Salome, (who was both Herod's grand-niece and stepdaughter), danced before Herod. In return, he offered to do any favor she might ask. Herodias tells Salome to ask for the head of John the Baptist, which is delivered to her on a platter. It is a disturbing scene.

"And immediately the king sent an executioner, and commanded his head to be brought: and he went and beheaded him in the prison." —Mark 6:27

Clearly, Jesus did not kill John the Baptist.

Conversation Questions:

- How would you defend Jesus against someone who said that He was violent or a killer?

- Have you ever gotten angry, like Herodias, because someone tried to tell you the truth? How could you handle it differently in the future?

The Bible

Old-School Video Games

THE BIBLE DID not make an appearance in many video games before 1995, but there were a few games that managed to sneak it in despite the Nintendo Video Game Guidelines.

The Legend of Zelda on the Nintendo Entertainment System was a ground-breaking game in many aspects, and it has since blossomed into one of the most recognizable and profitable franchises. Alongside the creation of *Mario*, the *Zelda* games have cemented creator Shigeru Miyamoto as a household name for many gamers. *Zelda's* influence on gameplay is still seen today, even beyond its own series, in games such as *The Binding of Isaac* (see Chapter 4).

In that first *Zelda* journey to the land of Hyrule in 1987, the hero, Link, uses an item called "The Book of Magic." However, a closer look at the original Japanese translation of the game reveals that the book is actually called the "Bible"! The Bible was just another item used to defeat enemies. This is a common use for the Bible in classic video games. In the *Castlevania* series, another seminal franchise in the video game industry, the Bible is used to help defeat Dracula.

These are not biblically accurate stories, or even biblically inspired stories, but it is worth noting that the Bible itself was at least seen as a helpful tool in defeating evil. After 1995, things changed.

New-School Video Games

Perception of the Bible shifted from a tool to destroy evil to a book used to harm, control, or repress the innocent. It is now depicted as a book primarily used by corrupt people in positions of power to spread lies among the people.

A sampling of games across genres demonstrates the pervasiveness of this view. In *Xenogears* for the Playstation, the "Word of God" is re-imagined as a weapon of mass destruction (see Chapter 6.) In *Final Fantasy Tactics*, a character named Alazlam J. Durai seeks to reveal the story of an unknown character, whose attempt to protect the truth was covered up by the Church.

Even the *Castlevania* series changed after 1995. Released in 1997, *Castlevania: Symphony of the Night* was the fourteenth *Castlevania* game released and is widely regarded as the best of the series. Rather than defeating Dracula with the Bible, Dracula himself actually quotes Scripture in this game!

Dracula's response to the playable character:

> "Ah… sarcasm 'For what profit is it to man if he gains the world, and loses his own soul'? Matthew 16:26 I believe."

Apparently, Dracula reads and studies his Bible. It is a disturbing scene, to say the least, and is reminiscent of Satan's use of Scripture during the temptation of Christ.[1] It is also a strong reminder that just like Jesus Himself, Christians must know the Bible well enough to defend it and defend themselves. The attacks from games on the Bible are not unique to video games, but they have grown more common.

---

1.   Matthew 4:1-11

The Da Vinci Code

System: Playstation 2, Xbox, PC, Mobile Phone
Rating: T
Year: 2006
Publisher: 2K Games
Developer: The Collective, Inc.

The Da Vinci Code is a well-known and highly controversial novel and film that had everyone inside and outside the church buzzing about the validity of the Bible at the time of its release. The video game garnered much less attention, yet the messages were just as strong.

The Content:

The video game player controls Robert Langdon, a professor at Harvard University. He is brought by the police to examine the body of Jacques Sauniere, a museum curator who has left clues to the true location of the Holy Grail.

Most of the game is spent aimlessly wandering around churches, art galleries, and museums hoping to stumble across an object of interest. While inspecting the various artifacts, the professor makes informational comments, presenting them as fact. While looking at a picture of Jesus being crucified, the character makes this statement:

> "The Gospels of Matthew, Mark, Luke, and John all tell of Jesus' death on the cross. They also agree that Jesus called out 'God, God, why have you forsaken me?' It's obvious to me that someone calling this out is not a god. But it's also irrelevant. Jesus was a good man, and He died because of politics, not because He did anyone harm."

Later, when examining a piece of art depicting a grave, the professor remarks:

"The burial of Jesus is covered in the gospels, but only Mark and Matthew mention that both Mary His mother and Mary Magdalene were there. It's funny how the Bible is written from so many contradicting points of view, yet people still believe it to be true, word for word."

The Challenge:

Does the Bible contradict itself? Does the Bible really say that Jesus is God?

These statements are an open attack on the Bible's claims about the nature of Jesus Christ as well as the reliability of the Bible. These are challenging questions, but Christians should not fear them! Nor should we suggest that it is inappropriate to ask the question. The more significant issue here is that rather than asking a question, for which we can seek a scriptural answer, the game has instead presented truth statements that directly oppose the words of the Bible.

Take one step back from the statements presented and the underlying questions become clear: Does the Bible contradict itself about the women present at Jesus' tomb? Does the Bible really say Jesus was God, or was He just a good man?

The Answers:

Does the Bible contradict itself about the women at the tomb?

The short answer is no. But before answering this question, it is important to look at the verses in each book and let them speak for themselves. Notice that none of them directly say that "Mary the mother of Jesus" was there as the game stated.

"Mary Magdalene and the other Mary went to look at the tomb." —Matthew 28:1b

"Mary Magdalene, Mary the mother of James, and Salome bought spices, so that they might go to anoint

Jesus' body." —*Mark 16:1b*

"On the first day of the week, very early in the morn-
ing, the women took the spices they had prepared and
went to the tomb." —*Luke 24:1*

"Early on the first day of the week, while it was still
dark, Mary Magdalene went to the tomb..."
—*John 20:1a*

While *The Da Vinci Code* claims that only Mark and Matthew mention two Mary's, Luke clearly does so as well. In the
same chapter, a few verses later it says who the "women" of
Luke 24:1 are:

"It was Mary Magdalene, Joanna, Mary the mother of
James, and the others with them who told this to the
apostles." —*Luke 24:10b*

The "other Mary" of Matthew probably refers to Mary the
mother of James as well, as she was mentioned as a witness
to Jesus' death in Matthew 27:56. So while the game claims
that Matthew and Mark speak of Mary Magdalene and Mary
the mother of Jesus, in reality the texts actually speak of Mary
Magdalene and Mary the mother of James, among others.
There is the possibility that "Mary the mother of James" could
refer to Jesus' mother, as He had a brother named James
(who wrote the New Testament book of James), but even if
this were the case, we see that this woman has indeed been
mentioned in Mark and Luke as well. Therefore, the challenge
falls flat.

This is not merely a misinterpretation or a case of mistaken
Marys. It disregards (at best) or distorts (at worst) the facts as
presented in Scripture. Even though John doesn't mention another Mary, that doesn't mean she wasn't there. A quick look at
John 20:2, when Mary Magdalene reports to Simon Peter what

she has seen, reveals that she indeed had company:

> *"They have taken away the Lord out of the tomb, and*
> *we do not know where they have laid Him."*
> *—John 20:2*

Her use of "we" shows that there was more than one person there. From these passages we know there were certainly more women present than the two the game mentions! Mary Magdalene, Mary the mother of James, Salome, Joanna, and others were all there! Rather than contradicting itself, each passage from the Gospels presents a different perspective of the same event offering a fuller picture of what that glorious morning was like through the experience of individuals who knew Jesus and who were there.

Was Jesus God? Or was He really just a good man?

If we believe the Bible is reliable, and we believe its claims are true, then this answer is as simple as seeing what Jesus says about Himself in the Bible.

While politics no doubt played into the people's cries for the crucifixion of Jesus and Pilate's surrender to their whim, that is a narrow view of the events surrounding Jesus' death. This view plays upon the non-committal tendencies of a secular worldview, downplaying the importance of Jesus' life while attempting to avoid complete denial of His existence. Many people would be willing to take Jesus as a good man but not as God. This option removes the necessity of making a decision about the spiritual nature of Jesus' teaching. The Bible makes it clear, however, that Jesus was more than just a good man. The Bible says that He is the Son of God.

> *"In the beginning was the Word [Jesus], and the Word*
> *was with God, and the Word was God." —John 1:1*

> *"But these are written that you may believe that Jesus*

is the Christ, the Son of God; and that by believing you
may have life in His Name." —John 20:31

Even the contemporaries of Jesus knew that He made this claim about Himself. Jesus knew, as did the teachers of the law, that only God can forgive sins. By offering forgiveness to the paralyzed man in Mark 2, Jesus is demonstrating the truth that He is fully God and therefore has God's authority to forgive sin.

When Jesus saw their faith, He said to the paralyzed
man, "Son, your sins are forgiven." Now some teach-
ers of the law were sitting there, thinking to them-
selves, "Why does this fellow talk like that? He's blas-
pheming! Who can forgive sins but God alone?"
—Mark 2:5-7

In his book *Mere Christianity*, Christian author and former atheist, C.S. Lewis, made the argument that we cannot consider Jesus a great moral teacher or a good man while also refuting His claims to be God. One will not withstand the other. Either He is a liar (and thus not a good or moral person), or He is a lunatic to think that He, a normal man, is God! Neither of these line up with the words of the Bible. The only remaining option is that Jesus is in fact the Lord God, just as He said.

The implication by *The Da Vinci Code* that calling out to God means He must not be God Himself is a misunderstanding of the nature of God that we see in Scripture. We know that He is the one true God, eternally existing in three persons (for which we use the term Trinity): God the Father (to whom Jesus cried out), God the Son (Jesus Himself), and God the Holy Spirit.[2] Most importantly, though they came into play in the events surrounding His death. Jesus didn't die for mere political reasons; Jesus Christ died to take the punishment for our sins so that we may have eternal life.

---

2.   Romans 8:9-10 and 1 Peter 1:2 are two examples that show us the unity and the function of God in three persons.

"And He Himself bore our sins in His body on the cross, so that we might die to sin and live to righteousness; for by His wounds you were healed."
— 1 Peter 2:24

Assassin's Creed

System: Playstation 3, Xbox 360, PC
Rating: M
Year: 2006
Publisher: Ubisoft
Developer: Ubisoft Montreal

The *Assassin's Creed* series has become the best-selling product for developer Ubisoft and one of the best-selling game series overall in recent years. Fans of the series are very protective of the game and defend it adamantly against assertions that there is spiritual controversy in its code. "It's just a game," right? Yet it was also named one of the most educational games of the year by *Gamer Magazine*, something gamers point to when they argue for the value of games ("Don't worry mom, I'm actually learning!") As gamers, we sometimes want to have our cake and eat it too! We have to realize that if we commend a game for teaching history, we have to be open to the idea that it might also be teaching religion!

The game begins by offering the gamer a self-conscious disclaimer: "Inspired by historical events and characters. This work of fiction was designed, developed and produced by a multicultural team of various religious faiths and beliefs."

You know this is going to be good… The game has not even begun, and already the audience is being prepared for the "tolerant" secular worldview and a not-so-subtle plea to the gamer not to be offended. It is as if the developer wants to tell the player: "Your faith is represented here, so don't worry, everything is fine." While we respect the attempt on behalf of the developers to be considerate of various belief systems in making their game, it also serves as an alert that there are likely to be spiritual things you disagree with in the game. Although they may not be included for aggressive purposes, we must stay aware and be ready to test everything against Scripture.

Assassin's Creed takes place in the future, in the year 2012 A.D. (Remember, the first game was released in 2006.) Desmond Miles is an ancestor to a former Assassin named Altair. He is being held against his will by Abstergo Industries, a corporation run by modern-day Templars, cross-bearing enemies of the Assassins.

Warren Vidic, a disgraced scientist and a former Ivy League professor, is placed in charge of finding out the secrets of Desmond Miles' ancestors. He forces Desmond onto a machine called the "Animus," which lets him relive key moments in the life of his ancestor, Altair.

The game then switches back and forth from 1191 A.D. and 2012 A.D. In the past, Altair is instructed by his Assassin leader Al Mualim to assassinate 9 targets. While Altair believes he is killing the targets for some greater good, he doesn't seem to understand his leader's motives.

The Content:

As he proceeds through his missions, Desmond Miles is confused by what he is viewing from the past. It doesn't seem accurate with what he has learned in school and textbooks. Professor Warren Vidic explains to him why what he is seeing in the past doesn't match up with what he's read.

Desmond: "Some of the stuff I'm seeing in the Animus, sometimes it seems wrong, untrue, like the history is off somehow. It doesn't…"

Warren (interrupts): "It doesn't what Mr. Miles, match up with what you read on an online encyclopedia, what your high school history teacher taught you? Let me ask you, do these supposed experts have access to secret knowledge kept secret from the rest of us?"

Desmond: "There are books, letters, documents, all sorts of source materials from back then. Some of it seems to contradict what the Animus is showing me."

Warren: "Anyone can write a book. And they can put whatever they want on its pages. Anything. Used to be we thought the world was flat."

Desmond: "Some people still do."

Warren: "Yes, and they publish books about it. Or that the moon landing was a hoax. I believe there's a book that claims the world was created in seven days. A best-seller too."

Desmond: "Where is this going?"

Warren: "The point I suppose is that you shouldn't trust everything you hear, everything you read. What's that your ancestors said? Nothing is true…"

Desmond: "everything is permitted."

Meanwhile, Altair continues to assassinate the 9 targets given to him by his teacher Al Mualim. After finishing his task, he discovers that he was being manipulated the entire time so that Al Mualim could gain the power of "The Piece of Eden", a powerful weapon used to brainwash people. This "weapon" is a correlation to the Word of God. Altair can see through the lies of this weapon, however. In the final showdown between Altair and Al Mualim, Altair asks why the Piece of Eden does not affect him.

Mualim: "You are not like the others. You saw through

the illusion."

Altair: "Illusion?"

Mualim: "That's all it's ever done. This Templar treasure, this piece of Eden, this word of God. You understand now? The Red Sea was never parted, water never turned to wine, it was not the imaginations of Eris that spawned the Trojan War. But this, illusions. All of them."

Altair: "What you plan is no less an illusion. To force men to follow you against their will."

The Challenge:
Is the Bible accurate? Can it be trusted? Is the Bible just an illusion used to brainwash people?

Warren makes an open challenge not only to the accuracy of the Bible but also to its reliability. He mentions it almost casually as a ridiculous example of a book no thinking person could believe. Interestingly, even this jab demonstrates the script writer's limited knowledge of Scripture. He comments that the Bible claims the world was created in seven days, but Genesis 1 says it was created in only six days! On the seventh day God rested.

Nonetheless, the challenge is an important one as it has become one of the most common objections to Scripture. Why should people trust a book full of contradictions and misinformation that has been manipulated over centuries? Many people imagine that the translation of the Bible is like the children's game "Telephone" where a message slowly becomes nearly unrecognizable as its content is changed, intentionally or otherwise, over the course of multiple re-tellings. The truth of the matter is far more reassuring, and demonstrates God's preservation of His divinely inspired Word through history.

The Answers:

Is the Bible accurate? Can the Bible be trusted?

Both *Assassin's Creed* and *The Da Vinci Code* raise this challenge. At the core, the question is whether it is reasonable to believe that the Bible can be trusted. The Bible's accuracy is confirmed by history (archeology and prophecy) as well as miracles. We will stick to the historical confirmation in this section. The Bible presents a reliable historical record and claims to be accurate.

> *"Many have undertaken to draw up an account of the things that have been fulfilled among us, just as they were handed down to us by those who from the first were eyewitnesses and servants of the word. Therefore, since I myself have carefully investigated everything from the beginning, it seemed good also to me to write an orderly account for you, most excellent Theophilus, so that you may know the certainty of the things you have been taught." – Luke 1:1-4*

Because the Bible claims to be historically accurate, it could be disregarded if proven otherwise. It is written as history and contains many verifiable historical facts that are confirmed by contemporary secular sources. If it were an attempt at "illusion" the authors would certainly have left these details vague so that any other historian or seeker would have only indefinite clues to its time and place. This would be more difficult to disprove. Yet both the Old and New Testaments consistently use detailed names and places to set the historical stage.

Many times, even centuries after the words in the Bible were written, archaeology catches up and verifies accounts recorded in God's Word! Take, for example, the Hittite people described in the Old Testament, or one of their kings, Sargon. Both were considered to be the stuff of legends, despite the fact that the Bible recorded them as history, until archaeologists discovered evidence confirming their existence. There are many examples like this that give credence to the accuracy of the Bible.

Likewise, there are far more and far older manuscripts that attest to the accuracy of the Bible than there are for any other book in history, religious or otherwise. Homer's *Iliad* is the most well-documented secular work from ancient times. There are 643 manuscript copies still in existence today. That is an incredible amount! In comparison, there are over 5,366 Greek manuscripts of the New Testament alone.[3] Most of these include the Gospels, and the oldest of them are within a generation of the ministry of Jesus. The New Testament is the most highly documented book from the ancient world. *The Iliad* isn't questioned for reliability. How much more should we trust the Bible!

The Bible, as a historically reliable record, holds Jesus to be the Son of God. This is reported as fact just like all the other historical details, and includes eyewitnesses listed by name as one would expect. They heard His teaching firsthand, and saw His miracles, death, and resurrection. In fact, beyond the witness of Scripture itself, there are 39 sources outside of the Bible that also confirm over one hundred facts about Jesus' life and ministry.[4]

And this Jesus, the Son of God Himself, taught that the whole Bible is the inspired Word of God. Jesus accepted the authority of the Old Testament, and viewed His own ministry as a fulfillment of those Scriptures.

He said to them, "This is what I told you while I was still with you: Everything must be fulfilled that is written about me in the Law of Moses, the Prophets and the Psalms." —Luke 24:44

---

3.   F.F. Bruce, *The New Testament Documents: Are They Reliable?* (Grand Rapids, MI: Wm. B. Eerdmans Publishing Company, 2003).

4.   Gary Habermas, *The Historical Jesus* (Joplin, MO: College Press, 1996), chapters 9-11.

Psalm 119 echoes this truth,

*"All your words are true; all your righteous laws are
eternal." —Psalm 119:160*

The Bible is trustworthy. A secular worldview begins from a presupposition that the miraculous is not possible and thus the Bible must be wrong. This leads to misguided (if not malicious) attempts to undermine the Bible's teaching. On the contrary, the Bible is the most attested source known to humankind. It still requires a personal decision to believe that the Bible is God's inspired word and not just an accurate historical account, but one thing is for sure: the Bible is trustworthy. Don't let the secular worldview make you believe otherwise.

Does the Bible brain-wash people?

In the game, the Word of God is a weapon used to force people into blind obedience. What the world wants you to believe is that Christians blindly follow Scripture because they are forced to, whether by their parents or their church. People simply wouldn't follow the lies if they could see through the illusions, right? This objection is often brought by those who have seen a life changed by a spiritual encounter with God, but having lacked such an encounter themselves cannot fathom how the rational and spiritual can coincide. That's why we need reasons for hope, and the Bible provides them!

It is fair to point out that there have been many misguided religious cults who have painted a negative picture for our society of the dangers present when an evil and manipulative leader uses spiritual things to control others. This, however, is not what Christianity is meant to be, and it is not what makes the Bible so powerful.

We see in Scripture that a person cannot be forced to believe or put their faith in God. It is a choice, and one that many do not make. But for those who do decide to follow Jesus, what they discover is the truth that the gospel of Jesus Christ

> *"…is the power of God for the salvation of everyone who believes…"* —Romans 1:16

The Bible says in the Old Testament,

> *"We all, like sheep, have gone astray, each of us has turned to his own way."* —Isaiah 53:6

Through the Bible, God is calling us back. Not as spiritual drones, brainwashed into obedience, but into a loving relationship where our faithful obedience is a loving response to all that He has done for us, and to which the Bible bears witness.

Each one of us has a decision to make: will we choose to put our faith in Christ and follow what Scripture says? Or will we choose to go our own way? Even a brief moment in a game like *Assassin's Creed* presents us with an opportunity to reaffirm our commitment to God's Word and God's way for our lives.

Conversation Questions

- Why does it matter if the Bible is true? How can you answer challenges about apparent contradictions?

- What evidence is there that the Bible is reliable truth?

- How would you explain to someone the reasons that we can trust the Bible as truth?

- Read 2 Timothy 3:16-17. What is God's Word "useful for"? How does it equip us?

- Is it possible to believe that Jesus was just a good man? Why or why not?

- What other verses can you find that say Jesus is the Christ, or where He shows the authority of God? Pick a Gospel, like Mark, and highlight them as you read through it.

- Write down the names of three people you can be praying for, and sharing who Jesus really is!

4

Churches

Old-School Video Games

CHURCHES HAVE TAKEN many different forms over the centuries since Jesus first commissioned the believers who lived at the time of the book of Acts. Many traditions, denominations, styles of buildings, styles of worship, and theological differences have taken center stage at different points in history, but at all times church buildings were meant to be places of worship. The variations on this theme are nearly as diverse in video games as they are in history itself.

Biblically speaking, "the church" refers not to a building, but to the people of God—followers of Jesus. The word "church" comes from the Greek *ekklesia* derived from a root meaning "to be called out." It refers to those who have been called out of the world and into a new life in Christ.

While the religions in games are often fictional, in-game churches usually reflect the physical appearance and characteristics of Christian churches (crosses, etc.). Sometimes, the churches are directly portrayed as Christian with no real distinction between Protestant or Catholic traditions. Classic games often followed the letter of the content guidelines regarding religious symbols by changing the cross over a church to a different icon. Sometimes this was only done for the U.S. release, but other times it was included in the Japanese version to avoid having to censor or change the game before a U.S. release was possible. A recent example, *Dragon Quest VIII*, has an icon similar to a cross but with the arms turned up so that it looks more like a trident.

For their part, old-school video games generally promoted the overall positive role of the church or the "sanctuary." The church was a place of healing, a place of safety. It was the one building in town for which everyone had respect. Often in the center of town, it therefore served an essential function throughout the course of the game.

Take, for example, the video game adaptation of the classic Robert Louis Stevenson novel *Dr. Jekyll and Mr. Hyde* for the NES. In order to achieve the best possible ending in this game, your character must first succeed in making it to the church. Influential RPG series like *Final Fantasy, Dragon Warrior* and *Lufia II: Rise of the Sinistrals* utilize the church as a place of healing where your character can recover from their injuries.

This is also true in one of the most influential Zelda titles, *The Legend of Zelda: A Link to the Past*. In the Japanese version of this game, the villain is originally a priest, but Princess Zelda finds safe haven in "the Church." In the English version of the game, the villain was merely a wizard, and the church was renamed "the Sanctuary," but the thrust is the same: the church is a place of safety from evil.

However, where once the church building was a haven to the player, these days the church isn't so safe anymore.

New-School Video Games

The representation of churches in video games has changed a lot over the years. This reflects not only the shift to decrease the censorship described above, but also an increasingly negative view of the church as an institution in our broader cultural climate.

Bloodrayne, released on the Playstation 2 in 2002, places the very first battle inside a church. You battle hordes of zombies, and by the time you are finished the church is not a place of worship, but a bloody mess. It gets worse. Later in the game there is another fight inside a church in which you battle a Ku Klux Klan member who is "preaching" from the pulpit with a machine gun. This would seem to demonstrate one of two things about the game's creators: either a deep-seated negative bias toward the church in their own life or an almost impossible lack of awareness of the true purpose of the church, to the point that it has become merely another set piece to be used and discarded. The popularity of *Bloodrayne* is such that it has spawned multiple sequels and a movie by the same name.

Instead of a place of healing or safety, churches have become a backdrop for violence and any manner of pseudo-spiritual religious events. Why do game-makers take this approach to the church?

Another popular game that demonstrates this shift is *The Indigo Prophecy*, known as *Fahrenheit* in other regions. The game has sold over 700,000 units worldwide and has won several video game awards. Here your character fights a multitude of ghosts in his brother's church. At the end of the game, you hear a preacher on the radio talking about the end of the world. It's some gloomy stuff.

It is not surprising that there are many examples of this theme within video games as the concept of "church" remains significant to our culture even if it is devalued in secular circles. In this chapter, we will take on two games as representative occurrences of churches in current gaming.

Resident Evil 4

System: Playstation 2, Nintendo Wii, Gamecube
Rating: M
Year: 2005
Publisher: Capcom
Developer: Capcom

This "2005 Nintendo Power Game of the Year" and critically acclaimed video game features Leon Kennedy, the hero from an earlier *Resident Evil* game, as he attempts to save the U.S. President's daughter, Ashley Graham, from a mysterious cult.

Resident Evil, as a series, is credited with both reviving and popularizing the "survival-horror" genre as its first release on Playstation was a dramatic shift in gameplay. Throughout the series the player is tasked with survival against impossible odds with minimal resources. It has spawned many imitators such as *Dino Crisis, Parasite Eve*, and *Silent Hill*, as well as a multi-movie film franchise.

Resident Evil 4 was in such high demand that the original Nintendo Gamecube release was also ported to Playstation 2, PC, and Wii, and high-definition versions were released for Playstation 3 and XBOX 360 as well. There is even a mobile phone version of the game. It has sold 7.03 million copies across these formats as of July 2011.[1] Since its release, *Resident Evil 5* and *Resident Evil 6* have also hit the market, but neither have matched *Resident Evil 4*'s success or influence as gamers and fans continue to compare its sequels to that momentous experience.

The Content:

In what is now often cited as one of the most memorable video game battle scenes ever, Leon finds himself surrounded by a horde of crazed farmers. They come after him with their

---

1.   Reeves, Ben (December 30, 2011). "Guinness World Records 2012 Gamer's Edition Preview".

sticks, axes, and chainsaws. As the horde bears down on him, all seems lost for Leon when, suddenly, a loud church bell rings in the distance. The crazed farmers drop their weapons, turn back, and proceed directly to the church to receive instruction from their leader, Osmund Saddler.

Eventually, Leon reaches the church and finds Ashley Graham, the President's daughter whom he is tasked with saving. Osmund, leader of the Los Illuminados cult, is there to meet him. He is dressed in a dark purple robe with distorted crosses on it. He interrupts our hero to reveal his grand and evil plans.

Osmund: I'll take the girl.

Leon: Who are you?

Osmund: If you must know, my name is Osmund Saddler, the master of this fine, religious community.

Leon: What do you want?

Osmund: To demonstrate to the whole world our outstanding power, of course. No longer will the United States think they can police the world forever. So we… kidnapped the president's daughter in order to give her our power, and then, send her back.

Ashley: No… Leon, I think they shot something in my neck.

Leon: What did you do to her?

Osmund: We just planted her a little gift. Ohhh there's going to be one h*** of a party when she returns home to her loving father. Hahaha. But before that, I thought I might bargain with the President for some… donations. Believe it or not, it takes quite a lot of money to keep this church up and running.

Leon: Faith in money will lead you nowhere, Saddler.

Osmund: Oh, I believe I forgot to tell you that we gave you the same gift.

Leon: When I was unconscious.

Osmund: Oh, I truly hope you like our small but special contributions. When the eggs hatch, you will become my puppets. Involuntarily, you will do as I say. I will have total control over your minds. Don't you think this is a revolutionary way to propagate one's faith?

Following this exchange, his soldiers burst through the door and a gun battle ensues.

The Challenge:

Is the church a place of violence? Is the church after money and power? Does the church brainwash church-goers (Christians)?

This brief conversation carries several common objections to the institutional church that you might hear in a conversation with a religious skeptic, a de-churched person, and even regular church attendees.

One accusation of churches is that they are primarily after money and power and only use the guise of "faith" or "religion" to deceive people into obedience or monetary support. Notice how this challenge is twisted into the threats that Osmund makes. In turn, Osmund clearly states that his religious followers behave "involuntarily" as they are under his control.

At this point, the game does not make an overt statement about the real-world church. Osmund is portrayed as a corrupt character, but what he presents is a significantly different and far more negative view of the church's potential corruption than games of earlier generations. How do we respond to these challenges from a biblical standpoint? Is the church a place of violence? Does the Bible call the church to seek power and money or to brainwash followers of Jesus?

The Answers:
Is the church a place of violence?

The church in *Resident Evil 4* is the scene of an evil preacher, a kidnapped girl, and a gun battle. It is a dark and scary place. However, it is important to remember that, biblically speaking, the church is not a building. It is not a place with stained glass windows and pews. A church is when two or more people come together to worship and learn about God.[2] It is a gathering of people called out from the world as followers of Christ.

This highlights an important fact: the church exists in the world. The church building is not intended to be a place of violence, yet it exists in a violent world. This is critical to understand. In turn, people who make up the church are called to perfection,[3] yet live and struggle in an imperfect world. Until Christ returns, we will be imperfect as well.[4]

Many objections are brought against church history regarding violence because of events like the Crusades, the Inquisition, and even exploitation by missionaries. None of these should be ignored, but they should not be taken as indicative of what Christ Himself has called us to be. Rather, they represent sinful departures from the work God calls the church to do in the world. So what is the purpose of the church?

Contrary to the accusations of Osmund in *Resident Evil 4,* let's see what the Bible has to say for itself and the purpose of the followers of Jesus who make up the church:

> *"His intent was that now, through the church, the manifold wisdom of God should be made known to the rulers and authorities in the heavenly realms, accord-*

---

2.   Matthew 18:20
3.   Matthew 5:48 "Be perfect, therefore, as your heavenly Father is perfect."
4.   See Paul's discussion of his own sin in Romans 7:14ff

*ing to His eternal purpose which He accomplished in
Christ Jesus our Lord." —Ephesians 3:10–11*

*"For the kingdom of God is not a matter of eating and
drinking, but of righteousness, peace and joy in the
Holy Spirit, because anyone who serves Christ in this
way is pleasing to God and approved by men. Let us
therefore make every effort to do what leads to peace
and to mutual edification." —Romans 14:17–19*

Even at times when Jesus says that He did not come to bring peace but a sword, what He refers to is not a call to violence for His followers, but the violence that the unbelieving world will enact on His followers.[5] Jesus Himself, however, came to bring peace to those who have faith in Him. We can experience this peace now, even as we await the new heaven and new earth when Christ returns.

The call for believers is to demonstrate the peace of Christ to others that more may experience the peace and life He offers. That is because it is not a mere man, and certainly not a violent villain, who is the head of the Church, but Jesus—who is God.

*"He is also head of the body, the church."
—Colossians 1:18a*

Is the church after money and power?

The answer to the first challenge should make this second challenge easier to address. We have seen already that the purpose of the church in the New Testament is to spread the good news of Jesus Christ, which is the power of God for salvation to all who believe.[6]

Why then is it so common for people to accuse the church

5.   Matthew 10:34-36
6.   Romans 1:16

of always wanting money? Certainly the Bible talks a great deal about money! From instruction in the Old Testament about how to support God's ministry through the tithe,[7] to New Testament examples of generosity from one church congregation to another,[8] we see that God often talks about money, because He knows it is something we deal with every day. He also knows that trusting in money easily gets in the way of our relationship with Him.

The Bible teaches us to put our money towards God's purposes, trusting God over money and living generously so that we can experience God's blessing. It never once says that our goal, either as individuals or as the church, to amass material wealth.

> *"Watch out! Be on your guard against all kinds of*
> *greed; a man's life does not consist in the abundance*
> *of his possessions." —Luke 12:15*

Instead, money given in obedient generosity to God supports church ministries (among other things) as it did the Levites and the Temple in the Old Testament. It also reflects the generosity of God Himself through His people as we live out the truth that our treasure is not here on earth but in heaven.

> *"Do not store up for yourselves treasure on earth,*
> *where moth and rust destroy, and where thieves break*
> *in and steal. But store up for yourselves treasures*
> *in heaven, where moth and rust do not destroy, and*
> *where thieves do not break in and steal. For where*
> *your treasure is, there your heart will also be."*
> *—Matthew 6:19–21*

Notice, for example, that Jesus did not ask the rich young man to give his money to Jesus but to the poor![9]

Okay, so maybe the church isn't after monetary wealth, but

---

7.   Genesis 14:20; Leviticus 27:30-32; Malachi 3:8-10
8.   2 Corinthians 8:1-5
9.   Matthew 19:16-22

what about power and control? As with the example of money, Jesus' earthly ministry and thereby the ongoing mission of the church was not concerned with earthly power either. Although some of His early followers thought He would raise an earthly empire, Jesus himself told them:

> *"My kingdom is not of this world. If it were, my servants would fight to prevent my arrest by the Jews. But now my kingdom is from another place."*
> —*John 18:36*

After the feeding of the 5000:

> *"After the people saw the miraculous sign that Jesus did, they began to say, 'Surely this is the Prophet who is to come into the world.' Jesus, knowing that they intended to come and make Him king by force, withdrew again to a mountain by Himself."*
> —*John 6:14–15*

These passages demonstrate that Jesus' intent was focused on spreading the gospel message of eternal life through His death and resurrection, not on gaining earthly power.

Does the church brainwash followers of Jesus?

We will spend more time on the followers of Jesus, Christians, in Chapter 4, so we will keep this answer brief in focusing on what the church's role is in instructing and guiding the actions of believers.

The church, the individuals who have put their faith in Christ, are charged with edifying and encouraging one another to live lives that honor God and make Him known to a lost world. A relationship with Jesus is not a call to blindly do anything a church leader says, but to prayerfully ask God for His wisdom even as church leaders humbly teach God's Word as God has charged them to do.

"All Scripture is God-breathed and is useful for teaching rebuking, correcting and training in righteousness, so that the servant of God may be thoroughly equipped for every good work." —2 Timothy 3:16–17

"If any of you lacks wisdom, you should ask God, who gives generously to all without finding fault, and it will be given to you." —James 1:3

Verses that deal with submitting to others are also balanced with verses that remind us that we obey God first and foremost and submit to human leaders insofar as they are in line with God's will, discerned through prayer and meditation on God's Word.

"But Peter and the apostles answered, 'We must obey God rather than men.'" —Acts 5:29

This means that we obey God and submit to earthly leaders when they themselves are being obedient to God and to guiding us to God.

"Obey your leaders and submit to them, for they are keeping watch over your souls, as those who will have to give an account. Let them do this with joy and not with groaning, for that would be of no advantage to you." —Hebrews 13:17

That challenge appears in many games. So be prepared to defend your faith!

Blitz: The League II

System: Playstation 3, Xbox 360
Rating: M
Year: 2008
Publisher: Midway Games
Developer: Midway Games

Now, wait a minute! What is a sports game doing here?

Sure, football games are played on Sunday, but what does that have to do with a video game? Surprisingly, the more parents hear about secular messages in video games, the more eager they are to dump all the games in the house… except maybe the sports games, right? But that would be too easy.

Without getting into the way that a wholesale game dump misses the point of this book, it is interesting to see how sports games are given a free pass when it comes to spiritual content and secular messages. Parents need to be involved in any kind of media that comes into the house, and gamers need to keep their eyes and ears wide open. Even sports games are made by people whose secular worldview can leak into the game's content and advertising.

NFL Blitz is one of the most exciting sports arcade games ever made. Seven-on-seven football with high scores, where wrestling style late hits are not only allowed but encouraged after the whistle and even an offensive lineman can play quarterback like Joe Montana. When this sequel of the game was released for the Playstation 3, it was a first day purchase for many gamers. A Christian gamer, however, might do a double-take if they heard this clip from a commercial for the game…

The Content:

> "Every Sunday when America goes to church, we go to war! While they pray for salvation, we play for survival! This is our cathedral, the game is our religion! And every religion has a judgment day."

The voice-over is provided by football legend Lawrence Taylor, who had a great playing career, but a destructive and broken personal life. Not exactly a role-model for gamers. This game, a family friendly arcade classic, now parades sport as religion in a culture that flirts with the idolatry of professional sports.

The Challenge:

Is church a waste of time? Is every religion the same?

The commercial wastes no time with insinuation, but comes right out and says "the game is our religion!" We are big time sports fans ourselves, but it is no secret that professional sports in the United States border on idolatry for many Christians. That is exactly the claim this commercial makes: stop wasting time at church, come and worship the game of football!

This is not a statement made as a challenge to God, because whoever wrote it does not seem to believe God is there at all, or they would be afraid to do so! The implications are that church attendance is a waste of time, prayers for salvation are a waste of effort, and that "every religion" is fundamentally the same, so why not choose the religion of football?

The Answers:

Is church a waste of time?

This commercial devalues churches as critical gathering places of Christ's followers. Whether they think this is harmless, that church-goers aren't their target audience, or actually intended an open attack on church attendance is irrelevant. The challenge is there. Video games in general continue to paint the church as a "bad" place, but that couldn't be further from the truth. It is a good thing when Christians get together on a regular basis, and it is necessary for our growth as believers.

"Behold, how good and how pleasant it is for brethren to dwell together in unity!" —Psalms 133:1 (NKJV)

"For where two or three come together in my name, there am I with them." —Matthew 18:20

"Every day they continued to meet together in the temple courts. They broke bread in their homes and ate together with glad and sincere hearts, praising God and enjoying the favor of all the people. And the Lord

added to their number daily those who were being saved." —Acts 2:46–47

"Let us not give up meeting together, as some are in the habit of doing, but let us encourage one another— and all the more as you see the Day approaching." — Hebrews 10:25

Is every religion the same?

A presupposition of the secular worldview is that religion is not based on fact but on superstition or emotion, and therefore that any one religion is not so different from any other. This goes hand in hand with the faulty (and genuinely unlivable) belief that truth is relative and what's right for you isn't right for me. Tolerance reigns supreme, and thus all religions are equally acceptable. This is one of the greatest dangers of the secular worldview as it reduces the saving work of Jesus to a mere preference.

Christianity is remarkably unique among world religions. In every other religion, the central plight of the religious person is their quest to find God, or the good, or the meaning of life, and people try vainly to reach up to that glory through false religion. In Christianity alone do we see God Himself reach down to us, in the person of Jesus Christ, and lift us up to His glory.

The Bible leaves no room for discussion regarding a plurality of religions, but states clearly that Jesus Christ is the only way to salvation. We have already seen that the Bible is reliable and we can take its word as truth (Chapter 2), so these words speak convincingly that God alone is God and salvation comes through no other name but Jesus.

"Salvation is found in no one else, for there is no other name under heaven given to men by which we must be saved." —Acts 4:12

"Jesus answered, I am the way and the truth and the life. No one comes to the Father except through me."
—John 14:6

"For you are great and do marvelous deeds; you alone are God." —Psalm 86:10

"You alone are the LORD. You made the heavens, even the highest heavens, and all their starry host, the earth and all that is on it, the seas and all that is in them. You give life to everything, and the multitudes of heaven worship you." —Nehemiah 9:6

Conversation Questions

- What is the difference between "the Church" and a church building?

- What is God's purpose (mission) for His people, the Church? How is this related to Jesus' mission?

- Why is it important for followers of Jesus to spend time together in spiritual community?

- Why do you think the Bible talks so much about money? (Check out Matthew 6:24 for a hint!)

- What makes Christianity unique among the world's religions?

- How would you explain to someone else what going to church is all about?

- Remember those names you wrote down after Chapter 2? Try inviting them to church this week, and let them see for themselves what worshipping together is all about!

Christians

Old-School Video Games

AFTER SEEING HOW many Christian references there are in video games, it may not surprise you at this point to discover that Christian-based characters make appearances as well! These characters are easily identifiable because they incorporate religious imagery (priestly robes, crosses, presence in a church, etc.). This is significant because they don the vestments and imagery of Christian heritage (as opposed to Muslim, Jewish, or some other world religion). The word "Christian" is rarely used, so in this chapter we will refer to these characters as "Christians" when it is overtly stated in-game, or "Christian-based" when it is made clear by imagery.

In classic video games, Christian-based characters usually appear as playable characters that can join your team. The *Final Fantasy* series allowed for a character in a "white robe" to join your party. This is understood to be a spiritual character as it comes from a tradition of RPG characters referred to by religious terms.

In the *Dragon Quest* series, a precursor to *Final Fantasy*, this character is even called a "Priest," who aids the party to victory. Their job, much like the role of the church in similar games, is to heal the other characters. It is even possible, as some video game historians have noted, that Link, the hero of *The Legend of Zelda* series, was meant to be a Christian figure because he carries a shield with a cross on it, uses a Bible as a weapon, and visits "Sanctuaries" throughout the game.

In these examples, we see that spiritual characters are based on historically Christian imagery, even though they are not called "Christian" in the game. Interestingly, while there were few examples of the Christian in old-school video games, there are many examples in modern video games. Now, they are much less subtle and far less helpful.

New-School Video Games

Recent gaming characters are much more clearly Christian-based, often appealing to culturally created stereotypes like the violent religious radical or the naïve zealot. Recent trends demonstrate that the spiritual character is far from a hero, let alone an ally, anymore.

Fallout 3, for the Playstation 3 and Xbox 360, is a unique game because it doesn't follow the linear point-A-to-point-B storytelling of traditional games. Instead, your decisions have consequences, affecting the outcome of the story. You can be as evil as you want to be… or as good.

In one attention-grabbing scene, your character wanders into a nice neighborhood, which seems out of place in this post apocalyptic setting. A family home in this quaint neighborhood has Bibles in it, crosses on the wall, and offers you food in the midst of your long and difficult journey. However, as you dig deeper into how this family operates, you find out they are cannibals who kill and eat people. Of course they are. Now, in the context of the game, any gamer would immediately recognize the actions of these characters as evil, but what does this say about this game's view of Christians? Even if these in-game actions are an exaggeration, they reinforce misconceptions that many carry about the followers of Jesus.

Another way this happens is with the misquoting and misinterpretation of Scripture. Do you know the Lord's Prayer? It remains one of the most familiar passages in Scripture.[1] And you better believe that video game designers know it too. Twice in the context of the multi-platform game *Gun*, the Lord's Prayer is quoted.

In the opening cinematic of the game, the main character is riding on his horse in an apparent attempt to escape a group of men who are chasing him. The voiceover quotes the Lord's Prayer. Well, part of it anyway:

"Our Father, which art in heaven, hallowed be thy Name.
Thy Kingdom come. Thy will… be done …"

BANG

At this moment, as the man emphasizes the phrase about God's will, he fires a bullet straight between the eyes of his pursuer.

The prayer is cut short for dramatic effect, and the implication is that this man believes he has the power to determine who lives and who dies as if it were God's will through his gun. Later in the game, a preacher who is also one of the primary villains in the game, chants the Lord's Prayer before killing an innocent girl. Both cases are clear examples of men seeking their own will, but claiming God's authority in an attempt to justify their wrongdoing.

Halo 3, an Xbox 360 exclusive, is an immensely popular and profitable sequel in that system's flagship series. It, too, has a

---

1.   Note from Drew: As a pastor, I have performed a number of family services, and the Lord's Prayer is exceptionally encouraging. At one memorial service of a decidedly irreligious family, I closed the service by reciting the Lord's prayer and was amazed when people began to say it with me! When I asked one of the family members where they learned it, seeking a spiritual connecting point, the response was "I don't know; you hear it in movies and stuff." Is it possible people learn the Lord's Prayer from games too? If they learn it from a game, how will they find out what it really means?

priest-like character as the villain. He is called the "Prophet of Truth." At one point in the game the protagonist, Master Chief, arrives at the base. His compatriots update him on the Covenant, the Ark, the Halo, and the Prophet. Notice all the biblical terminology! The Prophet of Truth then sends them a message:

"You are, all of you, vermin. Cowering in the dirt, thinking…what, I wonder? That you might escape the coming fire? No. Your world will burn until its surface is but glass, and not even your Demon will live to creep, blackened from its hole, to mar the reflection of our passage. The culmination of our Journey, for your destruction is the will of the gods! And I? I am their instrument!"

The Prophet of Truth is a religious character bearing all the familiar biblical terminology and claiming divine authority for their selfish, violent, and wicked behavior. At another point in the game, Master Chief breaks in and overhears the Prophet speaking in language rife with biblically inspired phrases like "all who believe shall be saved." And, "Though our enemies crowd around us, we tread the blessed path. In a moment I will light the rings, and all who believe shall be saved."

Though they are not direct quotes, we can see how this language is intended to sound biblical and closely parallels passages like Psalm 27:2–3 and Romans 10:13.

"…when my enemies and my foes attack me, they will stumble and fall. Though an army besiege me, my heart will not fear." —Psalm 27:2–3

"For everyone who calls on the name of the LORD shall be saved." —Romans 10:13

These brief examples set the tone for what is one of the most prolific religious themes in video games: the misconception of Christians. This is us. We are the ones represented here by maniacs, mutants, and madness. Whether an ill-conceived attempt at humor, or an all-out blitz on followers of Christ, what you are about to read is not accidental.

These games present the opinions and critiques about Christians by game developers who have experienced the failings of such people in real life through their own families, churches, or other media. We should take it as an opportunity to take a close look at ourselves, to ensure that we do not fall into these gaming Christian stereotypes. While they may be an exaggeration, they are usually grounded in someone's personal experience with a real church-going "Christian."

Bioshock
System: Playstation 3, Xbox 360, PC
Rating: M
Year: 2007

"*Bioshock* is not a game, it's an experience." We have heard these words spoken many times about this game that has gained critical acclaim for taking the combination of gameplay, story, and thematic commentary to a new level.

The world of *Bioshock* is called Rapture: an underwater city built by the industrious Andrew Ryan to attract the best and brightest to a world where science, medicine, industry, and progress could be uninhibited by the laws of society and "petty morality." Your character, Jack, is the sole survivor in a plane crash over the Atlantic Ocean that leads you to this sub-oceanic setting. You must explore Rapture without getting killed by the city's creator and ultra violent citizens. The player uses "plasmids" (powers like fire and ice) along with conventional weaponry to work their way through Rapture in an attempt to determine what happened there. It is a game awash with violence and gore.

It doesn't seem like the kind of plot that is particularly prone to having Christian characters, and yet they make surprising appearances because of the thematic focus on morality in the game. Unlike many games where morality is not explored and religious characters only show up in violent or brainwashed stereotypes, *Bioshock* gives more depth to the commentary on the value of religious principles for the people who believe them.

While it demonstrates examples of corrupted "Christians," it also reveals a subplot exploring what human nature is capable of doing when they lose sight of the reality of God. The intentional ignorance of God and His moral code is a demonstrable cause of the downfall of Rapture at some point before the beginning of the game. In fact, the city's motto is "No Gods or Kings. Only Man."

The narrative of *Bioshock* stands on the ideas of objectivism found in the pages of Ayn Rand's highly influential (and controversial) magnum opus *Atlas Shrugged*. It expands on many of the concepts of that novel and even includes references to her and her work in the names of some of the characters. Rand developed the core tenets of objectivism which holds at its core the belief that the greatest purpose in a person's life is their own pursuit of happiness and personal achievement. It is a self-serving philosophy and stands in stark contrast to the "love God, love others" mantra that Christians are called to as followers of Jesus.

Bioshock begins where *Atlas Shrugged* leaves off, with the best and brightest retreating from the world to a paradise where each individual can do as they please and seek their own greatness in industry. *Bioshock*, however, takes a very different view of what happens next. In Rapture, something has gone very wrong as the city has been destroyed, the citizens are mutated, and the powerful have gone insane. *Bioshock* makes the implicit argument that when left to our own devices with a "me-first" mentality, humanity's greed and selfishness lead to its violent downfall.

This is in stark contrast to Rand's philosophy, but surprisingly compatible with the biblical teaching of the sinful nature of humanity. Details of the game, right down to character design, demonstrate this inherent degeneration. In essence, where many games display religion as a corrupting force, *Bioshock* appears to argue the opposite: that religious belief may be one of the only things keeping us from total destruction.

So where do the Christians fit into all this? Set against this dystopian background, any "Christian" characters in Rapture are a part of its downfall, mutated and violent. Despite this negative portrayal of Christians, some have actually argued that *Bioshock* presents a subtle argument against atheism by implying that a loss of belief in God contributed to the disastrous state of Rapture. We will draw some of our own conclusions, but one thing for certain is that *Bioshock* is a game that provides intentional commentary on human nature and the role of morality and religion.

The Content:

Beyond the underlying themes mentioned above, *Bioshock* is loaded with biblical terminology, usually with some attempt to tie in their biblical qualities, but always tweaked or twisted for the purpose of creativity in the plot. For example, there are two essential substances in the game called ADAM and EVE, references to the first two people created by God in the Garden of Eden. In the game, they represent scientific miracle drugs that allow the player to mutate and learn new powers through genetic manipulation. In the game they represent humanity's attempts to wield God's creative power by improving upon His creation, just as Adam and Eve were tempted by God-like knowledge in the Garden of Eden. Of course, this hubris led to the problems that plague Rapture as experimentation drove the citizens to grotesque mutation and madness.

Even the name Rapture comes from a biblical term that refers to the timely removal of God's chosen people from the world. This name is used to reflect Andrew Ryan's belief that Rapture would be a paradise for those who leave the world of morality, government, and religion behind. The game also refers to various places and items such as Eve's Garden and the Lazarus Vector.

Although the game's view of human nature appears similar to the Bible's, we have more work to do to fully understand the biblical view on the subject.

A voiceover by Andrew Ryan himself speaks these telling words:

"I am Andrew Ryan, and I am here to ask you a question. Is a man not entitled to the sweat of his brow? 'No,' says the man in Washington, 'it belongs to the poor.'

'No,' says the man in the Vatican, 'it belongs to God.'

'No,' says the man in Moscow, 'it belongs to everyone.'

I rejected those answers. Instead, I chose something different. I chose the impossible. I chose... Rapture.

And with the sweat of your brow, Rapture can become your city, as well."

As you wander the dilapidated halls of Rapture, you discover crates upon crates of Bibles that were being smuggled by Christians into the city against Ryan's orders. It is difficult to tell at what point during the downfall these Christian smugglers arrived, but it is apparent that it was their response to the rapid moral degeneration, almost like missionaries. It is extremely rare for any game these days to be arguing for religion as an aversion to crisis instead of being the cause.

However, for those smuggling Bibles, Ryan reserves the ultimate punishment. One of the most unnerving scenes in the game is when the player comes across Christians crucified in the halls as punishment for smuggling Bibles into Rapture. Written over them is the word "Smuggler", and at their feet are

Bibles and crosses.

Many of these "Christians" have also succumbed to the madness of Rapture and become mutated themselves. Often you can hear enemies singing "Jesus loves me," and "Amazing Grace," just before they drop from the ceiling to try to kill you. What is the connection between the Bibles, the Christian songs, and this violence? Is religion a corrupting force? Is this an extreme example of the familiar accusation of Christian hypocrisy? Certainly these "Christians" are saying one thing (Jesus loves me this I know...) while doing something completely different! These characters are, at best, hypocritical and, at worst, violent killers!

At one point, Ryan even quotes Scripture from Ecclesiastes 3 to justify his actions in destroying Rapture and its people: "A time to build, and a time to destroy!"[2] Again, it is taken out of context and, similar to the Lord's Prayer in *Gun*, used self-servingly for actions incompatible with the truth of Scripture or the intent of the original passage.

The Challenge:

Is human nature fundamentally bad or good? Are Christians hypocritical and violent? Isn't the Bible just a bunch of rules?

Bioshock makes a pretty clear statement about the nature of humanity, and while it appears to line up with a traditional Christian view, we want to know for certain what the Bible says about who we are, how God created us, and what went wrong! This is foundational to our understanding of His love for us and the work of Jesus Christ.

Are the hymn-singing murderers in the game an accurate, if exaggerated, depiction of hypocritical and violent Christians?

In turn, the game presents (from the villain's point of view) the idea that God's laws and morality are like shackles and if only we were freed from them, we would find true liberty to do

---

2.   Ecclesiastes 3:3

as we pleased. Does denying God bring us freedom? Or does it make things worse, as the game seems to suggest? How do we back up our answer with Scripture?

The Answers:

Is human nature fundamentally bad or good?

Bioshock takes an unpopular view of human nature when it shows that human nature is fundamentally sinful. Most proponents of the various secular worldviews we face today contend either that man is inherently good or that good and evil are an illusion and we simply exist outside of any innate moral code. This despite the constant stories of violence, prejudice, lies, and more in the news (and around us!) every day. Are those "few rotten apples" spoiling the bunch? Are all people truly sinful?

> *"For all have sinned and fall short of the glory of God."*
> —*Romans 3:23*

The Bible says that God created Adam and Eve (the people, not the plasmids). He created them in His image demonstrating His love and their value to Him as His creation.[3]

> *"Then God said, 'Let us make mankind in our image, in our likeness'... So God created mankind in His own image, in the image of God He created them; male and female He created them. —Genesis 1:26a, 27*

At the moment of creation, Adam and Eve were living as God intended: without sin and in community with God in the Garden of Eden. Sadly, when tempted by Satan, they gave in to temptation and sin entered the world.[4] This is critical in understanding the nature of all of humanity for the rest of time for one critical reason—through their sin, we are all sinful.

> *"Therefore, just as sin entered the world through one man, and death through sin, and in this way death*

---

3.   See also: Gen. 5:1; 9:6; 1 Cor. 11:7; Col. 3:10; Jms. 3:9
4.   Genesis 3:1-6

came to all men, because all sinned… Nevertheless, death reigned from the time of Adam to the time of Moses, even over those who did not sin by breaking a command, as did Adam, who was a pattern of the one to come… For just as through the disobedience of the one man the many were made sinners, so also through the obedience of the one man the many will be made righteous." —Romans 5:12, 14, 19

To put it simply, we are born into this sinful nature and thus separated from God and subject to His righteous judgment.[5] The good news is that just as the nature of all humanity became sinful through one man (Adam), so all of humanity can be saved through the obedience of one man, Jesus Christ!

"But God demonstrates His own love for us in this: While we were still sinners, Christ died for us." —Romans 5:8

Stunningly, right after Romans 3:23 points out our fallen nature, Paul writes that we,

"are justified freely by His grace through the redemption that came by Jesus Christ." —Romans 3:24

Through Jesus we can be redeemed! Through the transforming work of Jesus we are forgiven of our sinful nature and experience new life. Though we still struggle with the temptations of the world, we have hope that our true victory will come when Christ returns. Even though *Bioshock* got the human nature part right, they missed the rest of the gospel message!

Are Christians hypocritical and violent?

There is no doubt that *Bioshock* depicts formerly religious people as cold-blooded killers. There's really no nice way to put it; that is what some of these video games are presenting. In *Fallout 3*, for example, Christians kill people in order to eat them.

5.   Romans 3:23

In *Bioshock*, Christians kill because they are crazy. In *Heavy Rain,* they are investigating a murder and their first suspect is, you guessed it, a Christian. In *The Binding of Isaac* the Christian is so crazy that she tries to kill her own son in the name of God. Believe it or not, this is just a small percentage of the games that have Christian murderers in them.

Are Christians really like this? If some of them are, should they be? We have to be honest when looking at ourselves that Christians are fallen people too; redeemed, yes, but fallen. This means we are often hypocritical and sometimes even violent. The key point is that regardless of the sinfulness that real life Christians struggle against, it does not reflect who Christ is or what we should do. Two verses in the New Testament demonstrate clearly the danger of acknowledging Jesus with our mouths while denying Him with our actions.

"The man who says, 'I know him,' but does not do what He commands is a liar, and the truth is not in him." —John 2:4

"They claim to know God, but by their actions they deny Him. They are detestable, disobedient and unfit for doing anything good." —Titus 1:16

Followers of Christ need to live in a way that reflects the truth of their beliefs and commitment to Him in order that those who observe their lives would see the truth of God present. Both of these verses demonstrate a dark reality for those who acknowledge Jesus with their mouths, but deny Him by their behavior, as these types of characters in games so often do. It is clear then that hypocrisy is not acceptable to God, even though it has become something of a stereotype for believers.

The challenge that Christians are characterized by murder is even easier to refute. Let's take a look at the Scripture shall we? You'll love how easy this one is.

"Thou shalt not kill." — Exodus 20:13

We just have to go to the Ten Commandments to see that God does not want us to go around killing people. There are many other sundry laws in the Old Testament that reflect this prohibition against murder, and we find similar admonitions in the New Testament. When we face these challenges from people, we should not respond with anger but challenge people to look beyond news stories and video game scripts to see instead what the Bible has to say for itself!

Isn't the Bible just a bunch of rules?

Bioshock reflects one of the great temptations of humanity: to separate oneself from a moral code, thinking it will bring freedom and make us carefree. However, the reality is, as the game suggests, that our fallen nature leads us into chaos. This is why God's truth is so important and valuable as a moral compass for our lives. Without it things are a mess!

When we refer to God's moral truth, we are including not only the Ten Commandments, but the instruction we receive throughout the Bible about how to love God and how to live in a way that honors Him.

"When you were slaves to sin, you were free from the control of righteousness. What benefit did you reap at that time from the things you are now ashamed of? Those things result in death!" — Romans 6:20–21

Paul here points out that while being a slave to sin makes us free from righteousness, that is not the kind of freedom we want as evidenced by its inevitable fate. Rather, we want to be set free by the gift of forgiveness that comes from Jesus Christ alone who fulfilled all the law and the prophets![6] This is what Jesus means when He says to His followers,

---

6.   Matthew 5:17 "Do not think that I have come to abolish the Law or the Prophets; I have not come to abolish them but to fulfill them!"

"If you hold to my teaching, you are really my disciples.
Then you will know the truth, and the truth will
set you free." —John 8:31–32

The Bible also teaches us what our newfound freedom looks like — a picture of hope that leads us out of the darkness of chaos.

"You, my brothers, were called to be free. But do not
use your freedom to indulge the sinful nature; rather,
serve one another in love. The entire law is summed up
in a single command: 'Love your neighbor
as yourself.'" —Galatians 5:13–14

We see now how real the sinful nature is, how important it is that we live righteously, not hypocritically or violently, and that in all things we are experiencing freedom by the transformation that God's truth brings through the gospel of Jesus Christ!

Heavy Rain

System: Playstation 3
Rating: M
Year: 2010

Heavy Rain was developed by Quantic Dream and features a unique story that follows four characters and their search for a serial killer. It made waves in the gaming world for its depth of character and the uniqueness of giving the player control over every day actions like opening a closet or closing a window. This more deeply draws the player into the lives of the characters and the suspension of reality.

The Content:

Norman Jayden is an FBI profiler who is sent to help investigate the Origami Killer. He partners with Blake, a police officer who will stop at nothing to find the killer. One of his clues leads him to a religious fanatic named Nathanial. They walk into his house to find crosses hanging all over the walls and ceiling. Blake describes Nathanial as a "God-fearing idiot waiting for the end of the world." Nathanial walks in and gets questioned by Norman and Blake. Nathanial is severely mentally unstable, and the implication is that this condition is intensified, if not caused, by his religious zealotry. When Blake begins to rough him up, Nathanial pulls a gun on him. He begins to rant...

> "You are the anti-Christ. I shall dispatch you to your father in hell. He is the son of Satan. He was sent to the earth to destroy us. Demon, you shall regret confronting the emissary of the Lord! You shall know divine power! Christ all-powerful, defend us in our battle with the forces of Evil. Protect us from the cunning and wiles of the Demon! May God Almighty manifest the power of His Empire and may Divine Power cast Satan and all the other spirits that prowl the world in search of souls into the darkest depths of hell."

You are the player, now choose: shoot Nathanial in the head, or let him live. In the context of the game, neither choice is a wrong one. Neither has an impact on other events in the game.

The Challenge:
Are all Christians crazy? Are Christians just waiting for the world to end?

Heavy Rain presents in this scene one of the most common insults atheists hurl at Christians: that you have to be stupid or just plain crazy to believe that an invisible God created the world or has anything to do with daily life. Certainly there are crazed fanatics in the world, but while these are a minority of Christians, they often get the most attention in media. Someone who walks into Planned Parenthood with a bomb is more interesting to the hardened heart than someone who reads their Bible at the local coffee shop and then volunteers at a food pantry. The exception becomes a caricature of Christians to the hardened heart. It becomes a joke to them.

A second challenge the game probably did not intend to raise but is worth considering is the concept that Christians are just waiting for the world to end! Is this true? How do we balance our lives here with our longing for eternity in the presence of God?

The Answers:
Are all Christians crazy?

The depiction of Christians as crazy is one of the most open attacks on our relationship with Jesus, despite the fact that developers may not do this intentionally. It demonstrates the permeation of this stereotype in society, as well as in the game designer's own life that they have come to the point that the "average" Christian is crazy. The characters they design are often radical, insane, and lead to the destruction of others by their irrationality. Sometimes this reflects the author's personal experience in a church background and their rejection of that tradition for various reasons. At times this plays out as a critique that real faith should not be legalistic or violent, but more often it belies a basic mistrust of faith itself.

Have you ever noticed a Christian in a game known for being tremendously sane? Much more often they only appear for the purpose of playing the "religious nut." Perhaps you have even been called one or felt the sting of being an outcast for your beliefs. It shouldn't surprise us that the world will continue to attack Christians as being crazy. The enemy wants people to write off faith in God as stupid and even insane. This attack is more akin to playground teasing and follows intentional disbelief. It represents a hardened heart that only God can soften.

Jesus spoke a great encouragement to the believer who finds themselves stereotyped this way for holding a genuine faith in His saving grace. Remember what He said,

"Blessed are you when people insult you, persecute you and falsely say all kinds of evil against you because of me." — Matthew 5:11

The reality is that we can't do anything to stop this, at least not completely. Truthfully, we should expect persecution! As Scripture says in John 15:18, the world will hate us. Don't let the insults affect you. Focus on God and respond to persecution with love so that you might show God's love to them!

Are Christians just waiting for the end of the world?

As Christians, we speak often of our hope for eternal life in a place where there are "no more tears."[7] In Philippians 1:21, Paul, a faithful follower of Christ, makes a surprising comment: "For to me, to live is Christ and to die is gain." He follows this up by admitting that,

"I am torn between the two: I desire to depart and be with Christ, which is better by far; but it is more necessary for you that I remain in the body."

We see in Paul's honesty that his greatest desire is for the day when he will again see Jesus, knowing that this would mean purification from his own sinful struggle and joyous eternity in the presence of God! In this sense, he can't wait for the end of the world (at least his own end). This could be extended to the anticipation all Christians have for the day of Jesus' second coming.

"So Christ was sacrificed once to take away the sins of many people; and He will appear a second time, not to bear sin, but to bring salvation to those who are waiting for Him." — Hebrews 9:28

However, Paul balances this with the fact that God still has work for him to do here on earth. The critical difference between the New Testament teaching through Paul and the actions of Na-

---

7.   Revelation 21:4

thanial in *Heavy Rain* is summarized in the letter to the Philippians:

"Convinced of this, I know that I will remain, and I will continue with all of you for your progress and joy in the faith, so that through my being with you again your boasting in Christ Jesus will abound on account of me." —Philippians 1:25–26

As Christians, we find hope in knowing that one day Christ's victory will be complete and we will be made perfect in His presence in heaven. So we wait patiently, but not passively! And certainly not hiding in our homes!

Followers of Jesus are called by Him to take up the mission and to share the gospel that He Himself proclaimed!

"Then Jesus came to them and said, "All authority in heaven and on earth has been given to me. Therefore go and make disciples of all nations, baptizing them in the name of the Father and of the Son and of the Holy Spirit, and teaching them to obey everything I have commanded you. And surely I am with you always, to the very end of the age" —Matthew 28:18–20

A wise man once said, "If you wonder if your work on earth is done… if you're still here, it isn't." We anxiously anticipate and pray for the return of Jesus Christ while obediently following Him. Know His word, live like He did, and share His story.

The Binding of Isaac

System: PC, Mac, Linux
Rating: NA
Year: 2011
Publisher: Independent

The Binding of Isaac. Do you recognize that title? If you do, it's probably from the heading in a Bible text in Genesis 22. If you read your Bible regularly, things like this become easier to recognize. This is an indy game (independently developed) that represents the growing availability of games and game production without all the costs and red-tape of larger companies and publishers. They face a more daunting task of promotion and marketing, but through downloading resources like *Steam* on the PC, gamers can rate and recommend games like this to one another, helping them to become cult hits and eventually best-selling titles. At the time of this writing, *The Binding of Isaac* is available on several platforms including PC and PS3 and includes an expansion that nearly doubles the length of the game.

This is one of the few cases where a game developer makes direct statements about the religious content of their game. Edmund McMillen, the game's creator, wrote a blog on the gaming website *Gamasutra* where he stated, "I wanted to make a rogue-like game using *The Legend of Zelda* dungeon structure, and I wanted to make a game about my relationship with religion."[8] (All quotes by McMillen in this section are from the *Gamasutra* blog.) So in case anyone says, "It's just a game…" It's not! Of course, his desire to make a game about religion does not automatically make it bad. In fact, it lends credence to the increasing reality that video games are part of our greater cultural dialogue.

Nintendo turned the game down when McMillen tried releasing it for the Nintendo 3DS, despite its success on other platforms. Their reason was due to "questionable religious content."[9] This "censorship" angered a lot of fans and gaming websites. Gamers who wanted to play this game on the Nintendo 3DS took to the web to write about how Nintendo was making a huge mistake. The game got very positive scores from the critics who also questioned Nintendo's decision, saying it should be the parent's responsibility to decide what games their children purchase.

---

8. http://www.gamasutra.com/view/feature/182380/postmortem_mcmillen_and_himsls_.php

9. http://www.destructoid.com/nintendo-wont-allow-the-binding-of-isaac-on-the-3ds-eshop-222917.phtml

When you see what this game is about, you may be surprised at the energy gamers spent on justifying it (it's just a game!) rather than protesting! Imagine the outcry that might follow if this game was made about other religions! How would people respond? We believe the response would be completely different.

Strangely, controversy can actually be good for sales! Recently, Christians were (supposedly) picketing another game, called *Dante's Inferno*. The "Christians" marched around and picketed outside of EA Games' offices. We put "Christians" in quotes there for a reason. A few days later it was revealed that it was all a publicity stunt. EA Games had paid actors to act like Christians (see that stereotype coming into play again?) to try and build up media hype. Christians weren't actually the crazed zealots after all.

Now, we don't think pickets or protests are the best way to express frustration over games, but we do believe we need to take a firm stand for God's truth and say "We will not buy this game!" Then, we need to be prepared to defend our faith and the word of God against similar attacks whether in this game or anywhere else we find them.

The Content:

The trailer for *Binding of Isaac* will give you chills. The scariest thing of all is how the Christian is portrayed. It is an intentional and acutely negative critique of Christianity.

Here is a transcript of the trailer for the game. Be warned, it is shocking:

"Isaac and his mother lived alone in a small house on a hill. Isaac kept to himself, drawing pictures and playing with his toys as his mom watched Christian broadcasts on the television. Life was simple and they were both happy. That was until the day Isaac's mom heard a voice from above.

(God speaking) 'Your son has become corrupted by sin.

He needs to be saved.'

'I will do my best to save him my Lord,' Isaac's mother replied. She rushed into Isaac's room, removing all that was evil from his life.

Again the voice called to her, 'Isaac's soul is still corrupt. He needs to be cut off from all that is evil in this world and confess his sins.'

'I will follow your instructions, O Lord, I have faith in thee.' Isaac's mother replied as she locked Isaac in his room, away from the evils of the world. One last time Isaac's mom heard the voice of God calling to her.

'You've done as I asked. But I still question your devotion to me. To prove your faith I will ask one more thing of you.'

'Yes Lord, anything,' Isaac's mother begged.

'To prove your love and devotion I require a sacrifice. Your son Isaac will be this sacrifice. Go into his room and end his life as an offering to me to prove you love me above all else.'

'Yes Lord,' she replied, grabbing a butcher's knife from the kitchen.

Isaac, watching through a crack in his door, trembled in fear. Scrambling around his room to find a hiding place he noticed a trap door to the basement hidden under his rug. Without hesitation he flung open the hatch just as his mother burst through his door and threw himself down into the unknown depth below."

Seeing how God is portrayed here brings tears to our eyes

as we reflect on the spiritual condition of a heart that thinks this is who God is! The first time we each saw this trailer we were left speechless and sad. Why does the world hate God so much? Our own moms, both of them Christians, played critical roles in guiding us to God's love, and their faithfulness helped us find the Lord. What would bring a person to have such a deep misunderstanding of the goodness of God?

McMillen, describing his own history with Christians, said, "I grew up in a religious family. My mom's side is Catholic, and my dad's side is born-again Christians." He goes on to describe Catholic practices as magical before adding, "… most of the themes of violence actually come from my Catholic upbringing, and in a lot of ways I loved that aspect of our religion. Sadly, the other side of my family was a bit more harsh in their views on the Bible; I was many times told I was going to Hell and [they] generally condemned me for my sins."

For McMillen, the "inspiring" part of Christianity is the violence (sound familiar?), while the sad part was reflected in judgmental behavior from Christian family members. This led him away from the church and informs the message he wants to deliver in his game.

We can sympathize with many who have had negative religious experiences in their past, which is why we always want to point them beyond the failures of people or churches around them and back to the word of God itself. Let Jesus speak for Himself and see what He says about truth, sin, love, and what it means to be a follower of Christ.

We are not perfect, but we pray that by God's grace and the Holy Spirit's power, our own families will see Christ in us rather than being turned away from Him.

The Challenge:

Isn't it just a game? Why did God ask Abraham to sac-rifice Isaac?

Some of the challenges here are answered in other parts of this chapter so we will focus here on two unique challenges. One is the seminal question of this book: Isn't it just a game? The other addresses the head-on challenge to God's relation-ship with Abraham and his son Isaac on which the game is loosely based and which McMillen believes represents the op-pression of religion in his own life.

The Answers:

Can video games really be that bad? Isn't it just a game?

Video games don't just have coincidental messages or truth statements. At times they intentionally set out to share a per-spective, challenge a social norm, or portray certain truth about the world. This is more common as gamers represent more of the general population and games have become *more accept-able for social discourse.* The Binding of Isaac is an excellent example as the creator himself has gone into detail (above) about his own experience with Christianity and how it informed the game's development. We commend his honesty, even if we disagree with his conclusions, as you will not get a clearer pic-ture of a developer's intent than this.

McMillen even notes that gamers themselves often miss this ability and intent of games. "I'm not saying everyone who played *Isaac* did so because they cared about these themes, or that they even understood why they were in the game, but I strongly believe that this adult conversation I dove into with *Isaac* is what made the game stand out to people and kept them thinking." He also comments at one point that the Bible is a "very good" book because of the fact that we can all interpret it in different ways. He has not thrown religion out completely, but, like many in the world, has turned it into a device that serves him, rather than a relationship serving God.

Is it just a game? Well, the game's creator doesn't think so, and neither do we! Like a book, TV, or anything else, games are what we make of them. We should never dump everything into one big "neutral" pile and say "it's just a game." If we do, we may be in danger of passively learning lessons taught by false teachers. Sometimes the messages are hidden, sometimes they are unintentional, and sometimes they are right on the surface. Regardless, we receive the challenge only to take part in that which is honoring to God.

> *I will set before my eyes no vile thing.*
> *The deeds of faithless men I hate;*
> *they will not cling to me. —Psalm 101:3*

Why did God ask Abraham to sacrifice Isaac?

The Biblical account of Abraham's test is found in Genesis 22. There in verse 2 God said to Abraham,

> *"Take your son, your only son, Isaac, whom you love,*
> *and go to the region of Moriah. Sacrifice him there as*
> *a burnt offering on one of the mountains I will tell you*
> *about." —Genesis 22:2*

Abraham then climbed up one of the mountains with Isaac himself carrying the wood for the fire. When they reached the place God had told Abraham to go, he bound Isaac and laid him on the altar. Even as he raised the knife, God intervened.

> *"But the angel of the Lord called out to him from*
> *heaven, 'Abraham! Abraham!'*
>
> *'Here I am,' he replied.*
>
> *'Do not lay a hand on the boy,' he said. 'Do not do*
> *anything to him. Now I know that you fear God,*
> *because you have not withheld from me your son,*

your only son.'" —Genesis 22:11–12

At that moment, a ram appeared which Abraham was able to sacrifice in Isaac's place.

Traditional interpretation of this passage explains how conflicted Abraham may have been, but that he knew there was nothing more important than his relationship with and obedience to God, not even his son Isaac. Yet, we also see that Abraham had faith that God would provide a way for Isaac to be saved if it was His will. In Gen. 22:8 he answers Isaac that "God Himself will provide the lamb for the burnt offering."

Abraham had already been promised that through Isaac the people of God would become a great nation, so somewhere in the back of his mind he must have been thinking "how is that possible if he dies before having even one child?" He had a promise from God and now a command from God that seemed to contradict it, but he also had faith that God would provide for both.

We also know from the prophet Jeremiah that God detests child sacrifice. Rather, it was a practice of pagans.[10] We realize then, that God too must have had another plan in mind from the beginning.

Reading Genesis 22 again in the context of the New Testament coming of Christ, we see an even deeper reality presented here. This was an anticipation of the coming of God's only son who would take our place as the sacrifice even as the ram that God provided took Isaac's place. Abraham even named that place, "The Lord Will Provide."

Abraham's faithfulness to give up his only son was a foreshadowing of God's own faithfulness in giving up His only son, Jesus. Hebrews 11:17–19 uses very similar messianic language

---

10. "They built high places for Baal in the Valley of Ben Hinnom to sacrifice their sons and daughter to Molech, though I never commanded, nor did it enter my mind, that they should do such a detestable thing and so make Judah sin." —Jeremiah 32:35

in helping us understand this Old Testament passage and the thoughts that went through Abraham's head:

"By faith Abraham, when God tested him, offered Isaac as a sacrifice. He who had received the promises was about to sacrifice his one and only son, even though God had said to him, 'It is through Isaac that your off-spring will be reckoned.' Abraham reasoned that God could raise the dead, and figuratively speaking, he did receive Isaac back from death." —Hebrews 11:17–19

Notice the phrase "one and only son." It is sometimes translated as "only begotten" and is the same phrase that describes Jesus in John 3:16. It was Jesus, the one and only Son of God, who was the sacrifice that God provided to take our place, free us from our bonds, and deliver us from our sin. God is faithful to His promises and to His plan for salvation.

Call of Juarez

System: Xbox 360
Rating: M
Year: 2007
Publisher: Ubisoft
Developer: Techland

Note From Carl: I'll be honest with you, this was a game that I was looking forward to when it came out. I love westerns! I love John Wayne and Clint Eastwood. I watch Roy Rogers and *Gunsmoke* with my baby boy. So when this game came out I was one of the first to buy it, and admittedly not for research purposes.

The Content:

The game features Reverend Ray, a former outlaw turned preacher. When he sees an innocent young boy appear to kill his brother, he prays to God about what he should do.

"How dare he end a life as righteous as my brother's.

If I could I would kill him.

Lord, is that what you want from me?

To be your sword? I have spent 20 years preaching to hyenas and wolves.

But maybe there are some who are beyond redemption.

Is that what you're telling me Lord? To destroy those who cannot be saved?

Is that what you want?

Then that is how I'll serve you.

And I will execute great vengeance upon them with furious rebukes.

And they shall know that I am Jehovah when I lay my punishment upon them."

This isn't even the worst of it! He goes to his church and grabs his Bible and his guns. When you look at the screen, you see a Bible in his right hand and a gun in his left hand. While fighting, if you press the right trigger button, the preacher starts reading the Bible. That causes the enemy to drop his gun and listen to the preacher. That gives you the opportunity to press the left trigger button on your controller, killing the man.

The Challenge:
Does the Bible ever justify sinful behavior? Is anyone beyond redemption?

"The Preacher" comes under fire often in games. Sadly, the challenges sometimes reflect real-life failings and sinfulness on the part of well-known Christian leaders. It is important here to point out that their failings do not characterize what true Christianity is or what the Bible calls spiritual leaders to do. These are sad examples of the fallen nature of humanity, and our desperate need for Jesus. One of the dangers in a game like this is the haste to stereotype Christians that undermines the trust the gamer may have in God's people who truly care for them. Yet the challenge stands, does the Bible ever justify sinful behavior?

The Answers:

Does the Bible ever justify sinful behavior?

In the example from *Gun* at the beginning of this chapter, the preacher quoted Scripture right before murdering the innocent. Here, in *Call of Juarez*, Reverend Ray misuses Scripture in his prayer in an attempt to justify taking revenge on someone he hates.

The reality is that anyone can, and many people do, twist, misuse, and misinterpret Scripture to serve their own desires. This is why it is so important to be one who learns good Bible study techniques and "correctly handles the word of truth" as 2 Timothy 2:15 instructs. We must never seek to pass off as God's command anything that is not found in Scripture itself. We pray that the Holy Spirit gives us wisdom to handle His truth correctly and find answers to the challenges of the world!

In the attack from this particular game, the Scripture is pretty clear. When Reverend Ray asks God if He wants him to be His sword, all he had to do was read what Jesus Himself had to say:

"You have heard that it was said to the people long ago, 'Do not murder, and anyone who murders will be subject to judgment.' But I tell you that anyone who is angry with his brother will be subject to judgment."
—Matthew 5:21–22

"The thief comes only to steal and kill and destroy; I have come that they may have life, and have it to the full." —John 10:10

Instead, Jesus says, "But I tell you: Love your enemies and pray for those who persecute you." —Matthew 5:44

Is anyone beyond redemption?

That couldn't be further from the truth. When you read the Bible in John 3:16, did Jesus come to save a few that weren't beyond redemption? Not at all. Who does it say that Jesus came to save?

"For God so loved the world that He gave his one and only Son, that whoever believes in Him shall not perish but have eternal life." — John 3:16

Jesus Christ came and died for the world that everyone who believes would be saved. His death was sufficient to redeem all of creation. He came to give us life, not to destroy us, and God alone is the judge, not us, and never for our purposes.

"There is only one Lawgiver and Judge, the one who is able to save and destroy. But you—who are you to judge your neighbor?" —James 4:12

Conversation Questions

- How would you answer if someone told you, "It's just a game!"? What example from this chapter could you use?

- How can you use "Know it. Live it. Share it." (Chapter 1) to answer challenges for yourself, and for other gamers you know?

- Is it enough for someone to try to be a good person, if they don't have a relationship with Jesus?

- Jesus died for us despite our sinfulness. Have you ever been accused of being a hypocrite? How can you point people back to Christ, even if you make mistakes?

- How does God's teaching lead to true freedom?

- How could you live differently in light of the eternal focus that God gives us?

- Pray that God will empower you to live a life consistent with what you know from His Word as you share the Gospel of Jesus!

- Who do you need to forgive and how can you point them towards the ultimate forgiveness that God offers?

Satan/Demons

Old-School Video Games

FRENCH POET CHARLES Baudelaire once wrote in a short story "that the devil's best trick is to persuade you that he doesn't exist!" The danger he warned against has now been fully embraced by the secular worldview of western culture. The devil, they say, is no more real than the Tooth Fairy and no more dangerous. Sometimes the image of the red-skinned man with horns and a pitchfork is played for comedy, a warning of danger, or even the "cool" factor. In this way, we have "given the devil a foothold" which God warns us not to do![1]

When devils appeared in classic video games, they were most likely the enemy, not a power-up and certainly not a friend. In classic RPG's like the *Wizardry* series, for example, demons were often the most vicious of the enemies to be vanquished.

In the game *Devil World* on the NES, you control a dragon named "Tamagon" who decides to "attack the Devil's World," which is about as deep as the story goes. The game is a virtual Pac-Man clone. At the top of the screen a large winged demon simply named "the Devil" dances around the screen. (Gamers in the U.S. may recognize "the Devil" best from the *Super Smash Bros.* series of games where he appears as a

---

1. Ephesians 4:27

trophy or special item.)

In *Devil World*, Tamagon must travel around a maze collecting crosses to help defeat the devil and his minions. After clearing the first stage, Tamagon must collect Bibles to defeat the Devil and send him to the next maze. It's not exactly the most biblically accurate portrayal of spiritual warfare, but at least the Bible is a tool to stop the Devil! Of course, in the New Testament, we see Jesus use the Bible to defeat the Devil, quoting Scripture to resist temptation in the desert.[2]

New-School Video Games

In *Devil May Cry 4*, released in 2008, you watch a character named Nero sitting in a church. He is bored by the preacher's message and instead listens to his MP3 player. This initially seems like a regular church, but then the screen shows the entire church. They are worshiping a demon called Sparda. The title of the series probably gives away that there is a major focus on the minions of Hell, and while this is one where Satan is still the "bad guy" it also shows that strange cross-breed of human and demonic powers at the player's disposal. The game is scheduled for a current-generation reboot in 2013.

The game *Brutal Legend* is loosely patterned after the real-life band Tenacious D and its star, actor Jack Black. They frequently employ the concept of the Devil as a truly "wicked" guitar player who will grant his musical ability to his followers. The game is filled with images of 666, devil horns, and pentagrams. They even say a mock prayer to the "evil, messed-up demon powers." Another music game, *Guitar Hero III*, glorifies Satan as the greatest guitar player of all time, to be defeated as the final boss of the game in an attempt to win back your soul which you sold for a record deal at the start of the game.

To echo Baudelaire, we see that the greatest danger in these games is that they do not take Satan or demons seriously. They

---

2. Matthew 4:1-11; Luke 4:1-13

treat them as fictional characters to be played for amusement. Yet even these games are nothing compared to those being released by a company called Atlus.

Developer Focus: Atlus

The Developer with Dark Themes

Demonic and Satanic elements are hidden in the recesses of almost every game developed by Atlus and across all ratings. Many times it is blatant, other times it develops over the course of the game, and sometimes it is hidden in secrets or at the final level. It is terrifying to consider what forces may be influencing the game development strategy of this company, but at the bare minimum it presents a frightening example of the outcome of the devil-as-fiction worldview.

While Nintendo did everything they could during the early 1990s to avoid anything controversial, Atlus showed no fear of the subject matter in their video games, especially when it came to the area of religion. Almost every one of their games features Christians as cult members and has Satan as a character. This is especially noteworthy in one of their tent-pole franchises: *Shin Megami Tensei*, from which series like *Persona 3* have spun off and gained popularity stateside.

"Shin Megami Tensei" translates to "Devil Summoner," so it was readily apparent that it wouldn't be the most family-friendly game, but what we discovered went much deeper than that. The game was released in 1992. The story takes place in Tokyo and demons have found their way back to Earth. Your character uses a "Devil Summoning Program" which allows the hero to converse with and recruit demons to fight for him.

At the end of the game, the player has to make a decision on how he wants to run the "new world." He can rule with God, but would be held under his strict laws. Or he can side with Lucifer, which would create a demonic world. Or he can decide to destroy both the angels and demons and create a world of true freedom, built by the hands of man. The game is packed with biblical allusions to things like "the thousand years" and the Messiah, all while challenging God's omni-benevolence and also His omnipotence.

While the game did not make it to the U.S., others in this series did, alongside many other Atlus-developed games. In Japan, the *Shin Megami Tensei* series is extremely popular. It wasn't until recently that this game became popular in the U.S. as well. How did that happen? Let's take a look at two of the games that did make it to America to get an idea of how seemingly innocuous games draw the player into demonic themes. They are *Trauma Center: Second Opinion* and *DemiKids*.

Trauma Center: Second Opinion

System: Nintendo Wii, Game Boy DS
Rating: Teen
Year: 2006
Publisher: Atlus
Developer: Atlus

Trauma Center: Second Opinion found popularity on the Nintendo Wii which offered alternative styles of gameplay with motion control. The game used the Wii remote as a tool for players to perform emergency surgery on game characters with the wave of a hand. It is a unique game, and players who were tired of the avalanche of first person shooters could find some variety of gameplay.

Note from Carl: *When Trauma Center: Second Opinion* came out for the Nintendo Wii, I went to the store and bought it right away. I was so excited to see a game that didn't involve killing others but healing. The game follows a team of doctors and they try to heal patients in need. Atlus couldn't turn a game like this into an anti-Christian video game… could they?

The Content:

The story of *Trauma Center: Second Opinion* takes place in the year 2018, where diseases that were previously thought to be incurable are nearly things of the past. The video game player assumes the role of Derek Stiles. Dr. Stiles is not your regular doctor. He is able to unlock a mysterious power called "Healing Touch" when things in the surgery room get out of hand. In order for the player to use the power of the "Healing Touch," he must wave the Nintendo Wii controller in the shape of a pentagram. Who is the main character drawing his power from? It's definitely not from Jesus.

Note from Drew: I bought this game for the same reason as Carl, but eventually gave up because I was terrible at drawing what I thought was a "star" shape. Having never beaten the game, I was completely shocked to discover what was hidden in the depths of this unique surgery game.

As the story progresses, Dr. Stiles must use his unique ability of the Healing Touch to cure a new disease being spread called "GUILT." Well, this is starting to sound a little more spiritual! GUILT is a group of man-made parasites that infect patients in the game. Dr. Stiles is one of the few doctors in the world who has the skills to stop this parasite. Throughout the game you heal patients while trying to discover the source of the parasites. At the end of the game, you discover that a character named "Adam" is the source that helped create the GUILT outbreak. Adam says that humans deserve the "blessing" of disease as he believes it to be God's will. Therefore he makes it his quest to rid the world of any doctors who would try to cure the outbreak of GUILT. After one battle with Adam, he says,

> "Your skills have given birth to many lives which never should have been. As it is written in Revelation 9:6, 'During those days men will seek death, but will not find it—they will long to die, but death will elude them.'

Just as the prophecy states, I have set a plague upon mankind to torment those who have betrayed natural law. …At the end of all life, I alone will stand as an angel before the gaping abyss… I, who have become the great destroyer Apollyon!"

Your character responds by saying,

 "Your medicine is deceit, and you are nothing but a false prophet…"

The character may be on to something by using that name! The Greek word Apollyon, means "the Destroyer" and it appears as a name only in the New Testament. Many commentators debate whether this name is intended to represent the anti-Christ or Satan himself, but one thing that is clear is that he is in no way a servant of God's will as he presents himself in *Trauma Center*.

The Challenge:

This game presents two demonic power sources. One is represented by Adam who claims to do the will of God but identifies himself with the anti-Christ of Revelation 9. Whether the game admits it or not, we know this means he is not doing the good will of God with his power. In turn, the main character uses the pentagram, a standard satanic symbol, to combat Adam. Is this then meant to be good? Again, the game does not make it clear if he believes he is stopping God's will or stopping a lying demoniac, but it is presented as "good" that he uses this demonic power.

The Answers:

Can demonic power be used for good?

This one almost seems too easy, but it is a legitimate question coming from the theological mess in this game. Many have worshiped false gods throughout history and even sought demonic powers to procure long life, wealth, or power. It is these events that are fictionalized in games like *Brutal Legends* or *Guitar Hero III* mentioned above. There are video games that encourage players to draw their power from demons, presenting this dangerous spiritual trap as mere fiction. The Bible, however, is very clear that we should steer clear of demonic influence as we consistently see in Scripture that demons only cause destruction and fear in attempts to drive us away from God.

Mark 1:26 describes an evil spirit violently shaking and shrieking within a possessed man. Luke 9:42 describes a young boy thrown to the ground in convulsions by a demon. In contrast to this, Jesus not only heals sickness and disease but casts out demons as well.[3] He did the same in each of the examples above, while Acts 8:7 shows how "evil spirits came out of many" by Jesus' power.

Believers are warned several times in the Bible not to meddle with demonic forces or to be deceived into thinking they can control them or make them helpful. Paul's address in 1 Corinthians seems to indicate that believers in the early church struggled with this same question: can anyone experience the will of God while glorifying demonic powers?

"What harmony is there between Christ and Belial?"
—*2 Corinthians 6:15a*

"No, but the sacrifices of pagans are offered to demons, not to God, and I do not want you to be participants with demons. You cannot drink the cup of the Lord and the cup of demons too; you cannot have a part in both the Lord's table and the table of demons."
—*1 Corinthians 10:21*

Instead, we rest in the power and plan of God by the blood of Jesus Christ. Just as Paul prays that we may know,

---

3.   Matthew 8:14-17

*"His incomparably great power for us who believe.
That power is like the working of his mighty strength,
which He exerted in Christ when He raised him from
the dead and seated him at his right hand in the heavenly realms, far above all rule and authority, power and
dominion…"* —Ephesians 1:19–21a

DemiKids

System: Gameboy Advance
Rating: Everyone
Year: 2003
Publisher: Atlus
Developer: Multimedia Intelligence Transfer

Earlier in this chapter we wrote about *Shin Megami Tensei* and how they had trouble getting the games to an American audience. The series was making a lot of money in Japan, but they needed to find a way to hit a broader audience. They found it by targeting children. *DemiKids* is similar in artistic style and gameplay to the immensely popular *Pokemon* series, only here the characters collect and level-up demons instead of monsters.

First of all, notice that this game is rated "E." That would be the same as taking your child to a G rated movie. Gamers often challenge us about games like *Bioshock* saying "It's rated M, children shouldn't be playing anyway!" We have already shown that many under-aged gamers get access to M rated games, and now *DemiKids* demonstrates that even games rated E can be packed with ungodly spiritual content!

The Content:

The very first scene in the game takes place in a realm called the "Dark Palace."

"Lucifer: What is it, Forlo?

Forlo: Lord Lucifer… Forgive me. I bear bad news.

Lucifer: If it's about the time rift that appeared in Dem, I'm aware of it.

Forlo: I thought you would be. You do know that if this rift goes unchecked...

Lucifer: All will end? You speak of the prophecy... I know it well: 'When the fabric of time is torn, tomorrow shall fade.'

Forlo: That prophecy also mentions children...saviors of our world.

Lucifer: I must know, Forlo! Find out if the prophecy holds true... If there's hope, find it!

Forlo: As you wish, my lord."

Wow. Right away they introduce you to Lucifer, a common stand-in for Satan, and he's actually a pretty nice guy in this game.[4] This opening scene shows his sympathetic plight to "save the world," albeit his demonic world. The prophecy states that some elementary students can help save his world.

The game then cuts to a school called "Rem Elementary" in the year 200X. You are introduced to your main character, Akira. Interesting to note is that one meaning of Lucifer is "dawn or light bringer" and the Japanese name Akira can be translated "bright or dawn." Even in the symbolism of the names the game

---

4. Lucifer has become an equivalent name for Satan in Christian tradition, although there is debate among Bible scholars whether the Bible ever ascribes this name to Satan explicitly. The term is found only once in the Bible in Isaiah 14:11 and describes the King of Babylon (also referred to in Revelation). It means "morning star, dawn, or light-bringer." Regardless, it is clear in this game that Lucifer is meant to represent Satan (just as he did in the classic literature of Milton's Paradise Lost or Dante's Inferno). Likewise, the meaning of "Lucifer" matches descriptions in the New Testament of Satan masquerading as an angel of light. The meaning is there, even if the proper name is not.

is drawing together the hero with the demon. Maybe you want to get even closer to the story. You can change Akira's name to your own.

Eventually, Akira gets together with his friends and has a conversation:

Akira: Hey Jin! Hi Lena! What's up?

Jin: Hi Akira! We need to talk. Lena says she's found something unusual.

Lena: That's right. I found… a book about demons in the school library!

Jin: You're kidding!? A book about demons!?

Lena: I knew it! The minute I mention anything about demons… Jin's eyes light up! I was in the library… looking for a book. That's when I found it. You won't believe what's inside! It's got a real spell for summoning a demon!

Jin: You're telling me this book's in the library!? Akira! A book about demons! Let's check it out!

Amy: Did I just hear you talking about… summoning demons?

Jin: Whoa! Who's this?

Akira: Her name's Amy. She's new in school.

Amy: Did I hear you right? You want to summon demons?

Lena: Well, why not? Have you ever seen one? If I had the chance, I'd take it in a second! That's what our little group is all about… Challenging the unknown! If you're interested, you're welcome to join us!

Amy: … … … … … … Sounds like fun… Count me in!

Lena: Great! Jin, Akira… See you in the library. Don't be late! Otherwise, I might just summon a demon myself. C'mon, Amy! Let's go!

Jin: Akira… Let's talk about this in the library, OK?

Your characters head over to the library and find the book about demons. They start reading it.

Jin: 'Nex, a wolf-like demon who guards the gates of hell…' Wow!

Lena: Jin is in a world of his own… He gets that way when it comes to demons.

Amy: … … …

Jin: Whoa! What's this…? You're kidding me? Akira, check this out! This shows you how to summon a demon!

Akira: You're right! Jin… Wanna give it a try?

Lena: This is so cool! Exciting, too!

Amy: Are you thinking about summoning demons? … … … … You need special powers for that. … … … … If you have those powers that would mean…

Akira: Powers? What are you talking about, Amy? What kind of powers do you need to summon demons?

Amy: … … … … There's danger in summoning demons… A summoned demon might attack you.

Akira: A demon attack? If that happens, we'll just have

to fight. Jin, we're ready. Let's try the spell!

The two boys chant the words to summon a demon.

KEYAGA KA LIKAHI REF ACHIMI MIYA…

We summon you to appear before us… NOW!

The Challenge:

Is the devil our friend? Is the devil all-powerful?

Now, we've included a lot of dialogue from this game. You may be thinking to yourself, "We get it! This game as a lot of demon summoning, it's bad! We won't buy it." But that's not the picture we want to paint for you.

Instead, imagine a parent, shopping around with their 6 year old child, looking for a new Gameboy game to play. The child grabs *DemiKids*, because it is rated E and looks like *Pokemon*. The parent, attempting to be responsible, looks at the box-art, it has cartoon characters on it. It's rated "E for everyone." No problem, right?

Parent and child go home, and as they go about their business, the child sits in the corner of the room playing their brand new video game. The parent has no clue that this is the dialogue their child is reading. Their young mind is being filled with satanic stories. And Lucifer in this game? He is a good guy. He joins your team later in the game. You want to be friends with him.

Now consider this: With what does a child spend more time: a video game or a Bible? Which will have the greater impact on him or her? Could they be led astray, deceived by the "fiction" of spiritual warfare to doubting the power of God?

Remember the *Shin Megami Tensei* series? Well, after they released *DemiKids* to the American public, you can now go into a video game store and buy all the *Shin Megami Tensei* series games. They are even remaking their older games for an American audience. One E rated game paved the way for the entire series.

That's how the devil works. He takes something evil and makes it look nice and friendly to get his message across, even to children. Is the devil our friend? Is he really an all-powerful force? An equal, but opposite, match for God?

The Answers:

Is the devil our friend?

The "goodness" painted on this satanically named character reminds us of Paul's warning that,

> *"Satan himself masquerades as an angel of light. It is not surprising, then, if his servants masquerade as servants of righteousness. Their end will be what their actions deserve." —2 Corinthians 11:14*

Lucifer may become the elementary students' friend in *DemiKids,* but that is far from the spiritual truth. Ever since Satan first tempted Adam and Eve in the Garden of Eden, he has sought the destruction of God's creation and the people God loves. Jesus knew this well and didn't mince words when He warned us against the devil.

> *"He was a murderer from the beginning, not holding to the truth, for there is no truth in him. When he lies, he speaks his native language, for he is a liar and the father of lies." —John 8:44*

It is a spiritual battle and Peter calls us to be prepared:

> *"Be of sober spirit, be on the alert. Your adversary, the devil, prowls around like a roaring lion, seeking someone to devour." —1 Peter 5:8*

Is the devil all-powerful?

A common cultural misconception, and one that Bible-believing Christians all-too-often share, is that God and Satan are equal opposites warring for dominion over creation. There are opposite comparisons to be made: God is always good and Satan is always evil. God tells the truth and Satan lies. However, there are characteristics of God that Satan can never match.

God is omnipotent. (Matthew 19:26; Job 42:2)

God is all-knowing. (Psalm 147:5; Job 28:24)

God is all-present. (Jeremiah 23:24; Psalm 139:7–12)

Satan is none of those things. He is a created and fallen being. He does not have the power or knowledge that God does. Unlike God who is everywhere, Satan is not in all places at all times tempting all people. So don't believe it when someone tells you, "the devil made me do it!"

Our own sinfulness is at fault as much if not more than the devil's direct influence. It is we who choose, like Adam and Eve, to give him influence or to follow Christ.

"The Spirit clearly says that in later times some will abandon the faith and follow deceiving spirits and things taught by demons." — 1 Timothy 4:1

This is exactly why Jesus came:

"He who does what is sinful is of the devil, because the devil has been sinning from the beginning. The reason the Son of God appeared was to destroy the devil's work." — 1 John 3:8

Contrary to the biblical account, at the end of *DemiKids*, Lucifer is saved from his destruction and lives happily ever after. The Bible tells a different story! It is not a tug-of-war! The outcome is already assured. Through the death and resurrection of Jesus, the victory is won and we share in the victory as faithful followers of Jesus! We can explain to our children that Satan does not have a happy ending in the Bible. It says in Revelation 20,

"And the devil, who deceived them, was thrown into

the lake of burning sulfur, where the beast and the false
prophet had been thrown. They will be tormented day
and night for ever and ever." —Revelation 20:10

It is by the power of Jesus that the devil is destroyed, and it is by the power of the Holy Spirit that we, His followers, have victory over the devil.

"Put on the full armor of God so that you can take your
stand against the devil's schemes." —Ephesians 6:11

"Submit yourselves, then, to God. Resist the devil, and
he will flee from you. Come near to God and He will
come near to you." —James 4:7–8a

Conversation Questions

- What are some verses that show us that God is all-powerful, all-knowing, and all-present? Can you find others?

- If God is all-powerful, does the follower of Jesus have to fear Satan or the demons? Why do we have to be careful?

- Why is it dangerous to think that Satan or demons are not real? How might the devil work through everyday things to distract people from God's truth?

- Instead of earthly or demonic powers, where should we find our strength, hope, and victory?

- How does the Armor of God (Ephesians 6:10–18) help us prepare for the spiritual warfare we will face? How can we fight back against temptation, not only from outside forces, but from our own sinful nature as well?

- How can you "test" the games you play (or your children play), even when the ratings don't help?

7

God

HOW WOULD YOU feel if a company made a video game about someone you love, but in the game they only said terrible things about your loved one? Imagine a game that talked about your loved ones, but all it said was how your spouse cheats on you, your children are liars, and your parents are deadbeats. What if the game told the world that your best friend hates you and steals your money? And what if none of it were true?

You would be pretty upset wouldn't you? Why? Because we protect the ones we love. You wouldn't stand by and say "My spouse doesn't really cheat on me, but… it's just a game." No! You would want the company to stop and you would tell as many people as you could the truth about the one you love.

Now apply that to games about God! God is bashed repeatedly through culture, games included. Do we get upset? We should! Too often we are so used to "tolerance" and letting everyone believe whatever they want that it stops bothering us when they attack the one we love! This chapter is going to explore the way God is portrayed in games, so let the challenge be on us to make sure people know the truth about who God is!

Old-School Video Games

There are two things that will surprise you in this chapter.

One is how frequently "god" characters appear in video games. These may be defined simply by an "all-powerful" streak or some other widely recognized god-like characteristic, though not necessarily referring to a specific god, or God Himself. The other thing that may surprise you is how frequently those characters are patterned, even named, after the God of the Old and New Testaments!

In this chapter, we will share examples of the first kind where they demonstrate essential characteristics of the God of the Bible, such as His omnipotence or His role as creator. We will also share examples of the second kind in which the video game character is designed or named specifically as the God of the Bible (i.e. the character YHWH in *Shin Megami Tensei*).

Many games, old and new, give the player the opportunity to "play god" in the act of creation. There is even an entire genre of gaming called "God Games" by the gaming community. More recently, one developer who has had great success in the genre, Peter Molyneux, has claimed he is on a quest to recreate the entire genre with his project titled GODUS.[1]

One such game is the Super Nintendo classic, *ActRaiser*. Often cited as one of the system's best games, it puts the gamer in the role of the "Master." It is your job to help rebuild a world that has been left in shambles. Tanzra is the enemy of the Master and wishes to conquer the world. You must restore civilization, fill the worship centers, and defeat evil. Your angelic assistant helps you on your way.

It is no secret that *ActRaiser* and its sequel, *ActRaiser 2*, are about the battle between God and Satan. In fact, the game is an intentional allegory for Christian monotheism in which the original names of the characters were not Master and Tanzra, but God and Satan (subsequently changed due to Nintendo's content guidelines). Like an old episode of *Dragnet*, only the

---

1.　According to the game's Kickstarter campaign on www.kickstarter.com/projects/22cans/project-godus

names have been changed.

The Master and Tanzra are fighting over the world. After saving the world from evil in *ActRaiser*, God and His Angel take a look at the world they helped save. They take a look inside of the "shrine," the people's worship center. What they discover surprises them.

> Angel: "……….. There's no one here. In former times, people would call for you and ask for your help. As cultures and lands become more advanced, do people tend to forget those who helped them? But then, people may be most happy when not in need of help from their master, or when they have forgotten him? Should we yearn for a time when people will no longer need to ask for our help?"

They find they are no longer needed as all suffering has been removed from the world, so they depart only to return at some future time when they may be needed again: a decidedly unbiblical conclusion. The ending to the sequel *ActRaiser 2* is very similar. It has a statue of the Master (God) with the following inscription:

> The battle between the Master and Tanzra is over. Tanzra has been destroyed. The Master has disappeared. Peace has returned to the people of this world. It's hard to believe such a nightmare ever existed. Time has passed… the grapes have ripened. A man looks to the sky and whispers, 'Thank you, Master, for giving us good crops this year.' Time has passed… the frozen land to the north is now covered with grass. A woman looks to the sky and whispers, 'Please help me find someone special.' Even though the Master has disappeared, people will remember him forever. The story of how he saved the world will be talked about for many

years. The Master will live forever.

On the positive side, God is shown as benevolent in this old-school game, reflecting a biblical characteristic called omnibenevolence which states that God is always good. On the flipside, he is also depicted here as an absent God, not invested in the daily lives of people who believe in him but only serving the single purpose of removing their suffering. Still, this is a far more positive spin than many games afford Him, and it seems to get progressively more negative as the gaming generations march on.

New-School Video Games:

Xenogears was originally released for the Playstation before being re-released as a Greatest Hits title in 2003 and more recently on the Playstation Network in 2011. In *Xenogears*, God is portrayed as a fraud. There are many examples of "preaching" in this game, but they are not preaching about Jesus Christ. In one battle scene, the character Jessie begins to preach to his son, Billy.

> Jessie: "Billy, you know now don't you? Stein's teachings were all a deception. That fabricated faith was just a worldly system for compensating those people with fragile souls. But, faith and god aren't things which are given to you from others, right? They are things you have to discover within yourself, and by yourself. Things that cannot be put into words, things that cannot be expressed… Isn't that what god is all about? 'Question not thy god, for thy god doth not respond."

Later he finishes off by saying:

> Jessie: "Your gun saved those people who were turned into reapers. It's not something anyone can do. The faith

that enabled you to accomplish that was no decep-
tion… God exists within you!"

In another scene, the boys head off to battle while leaving
two others, Elly and Margie, on the planet alone. The two have
a discussion about prayer.

Elly: "Anyway, we have things we have to do too, now.
And, while we do them, let's pray that everyone comes
back safely."

Margie: "To God?"

Elly: "No… To your own innermost feelings that everyone believes in…"

The theme of God's absence, hinted at in *ActRaiser*, is
now brought to light in *Xenogears* and soon becomes the very
foundation of storytelling in games like *Metro: Last Light* (later
in this chapter). In *Xenogears*, it is not only God's absence,
but His non-existence that is embraced in the pursuit of self-
deification not dissimilar from pantheism (the idea that God
is in everything). We cannot expect an unbelieving world to
avoid such topics as material for games; they simply do not
understand the reality of who God is. Yet it is critical that we
understand what God has told us about Himself through His
Word, the Bible.

To the unbelieving that sounds like foolishness and circular
reason to defend God's existence by using the Bible. There are
many arguments for the existence of an all-powerful being and
many more for that being to be the God we know from the
Bible. These arguments are treated in books entirely devoted
to the subject and in many brilliant systematic theologies. We
will here let it suffice that we have touched in previous chapters
on the reliability of Scripture as a source of truth which attests
to His character. This allows our focus not to be on logical or

ontological proofs for His existence, but rather on His words about His own character and His actions that show it to be true!

Likewise, if you flip through any respectable systematic theology book you will find hundreds of pages devoted to questions about the character, activity, and existence of God. We won't try to cover all of those topics here, but will answer in part a selection of questions that come up most commonly in video games.[2]

Metro: Last Light

System: Xbox 360, PS3, PC
Rating: Mature
Year: 2013
Developer: 4A Games
Publisher: Deep Silver

Metro: Last Light is the sequel to *Metro 2033*, itself a quiet hit released for several systems in 2010 and based off of a Russian novel by the same title. The story in the original game was set in the (then) near-future of 2013 when fictional Russia was victim to atomic warfare, forcing survivors into the metro tunnels to survive and avoid radiation. Those left behind mutated into beastly creatures called "Dark Ones." The game picked up some steam when made freely available as part of the marketing for the sequel: *Metro: Last Light*.

Metro: Last Light takes place in the same fictional future where humanity struggles to survive in the tunnels. Now, the threat is not only from the beasts without, but the beasts within, as people battle over waning resources and hopelessness.

The Content:

So far, the game isn't much more than another post-apocalyptic romp through an Earth-like wasteland. However, in promoting this sequel, the developer, 4A Games, made an interest-

---

2.   For further study on God and other questions of theology, Wayne Grudem's *Systematic Theology* is extremely helpful.

ing appeal to the very first page of the Bible. Official trailers for *Metro: Last Light* bear titles like "Genesis," "Salvation," and "The Preacher Trailer." The novel *Metro 2033* also had a Christian cult play a role, though it did not appear in the first game. The text from the "Genesis" trailer is an extremely accurate paraphrase of Genesis 1... with one notable difference:

Voiceover: In the beginning, God said let there be light to burn away the darkness.

On the second day, the sky was born, a majestic canopy for the earth.

On the following day, God sculpted the bountiful earth and planted it with trees.

With the fourth day, God split day from night and blessed the earth with the cycle of the seasons.

Then God filled the sea with life and set forth the birds to soar in the skies.

On the sixth day, God created glorious creatures. Chief of these were mankind whom He created in His own image. He blessed them, giving them dominion over all living things: to care for, to nurture, to rule.

And on the seventh day they say God rested. But God didn't rest. God left... or perhaps died.

Judgment Day came and He abandoned us, casting humanity aside like parasites. But there is still hope. We have to face this hell full-on.

Our fate I hold in my own hands.

The Challenge:
Is God dead or gone? Is there hope for humans?

This is a shockingly faithful paraphrase of the days of creation found in Genesis 1. Faithful, that is, until it gets to Day Seven. While the first six days accurately reflect God's work in creating and ordering the universe, even making mention of the image of God in humanity, the narrative takes a sharp turn from the truth at Day Seven when it asserts that God left, or worse, is dead.

Beyond this moment, and in light of God's absence, the character goes on to describe how and why humans must look to themselves, even he himself, for hope. Is God unconcerned about the day-to-day lives of people? Did He really just create everything and then leave us to fend for ourselves? Is God dead or gone? What hope is there for humanity?

The Answers:
Is God dead or gone?

The writer of this script must have had a Bible open right in front of them to get the level of accuracy represented in the first six days. That would mean every verse that says "God saw it and it was good" were also right there for the reading, including this one which says,

> *"By the seventh day God had finished the work he had been doing; so on the seventh day He rested from all his work." —Genesis 2:2*

Yet the narrator makes two very different claims, that God is either dead or gone. The idea that God is dead is an oft-quoted line from Friedrich Nietzsche, a German philosopher most students read at some point in a post-high school education. He states the matter thus: "God is dead. God remains dead. And we have killed him… Is not the greatness of this deed too great for us? Must we ourselves not become gods simply to appear worthy of it?"[3]

Here Nietzsche makes a similar conclusion that we are actually the ones in control, not God. Whether he attacks the existence of God Himself or more abstractly the loss of the idea of "god," or even the reaction against a personal God, the claim stands as one that lifts humanity above deity. This is not so different from the challenge that God has disappeared or left after setting the world in motion.

This game is not the first time people have claimed that God disappeared after finishing creation. An unbiblical theology known as Deism holds the belief that God created everything, put it in motion, and then backed off to let the rest of history work itself out without His help or interference. This view sometimes refers to God as a watchmaker, who winds things up and lets them run themselves until the watch stops. This view was popular at the starting point of U.S. history among many of the founding fathers who we hold up as Judeo-Christian champions ("In God we trust!"). Yet many held beliefs much closer to deism than to orthodox Christianity.[4] This meant, for example, that after setting the world in motion, God no longer revealed himself in a supernatural way. It would also mean the incarnation of Jesus never happened. Thomas Jefferson even edited the gospels, in what is infamously known as "Jefferson's Bible" to remove any references to miraculous works or statements of deity by Jesus.

Flying in the face of this challenge are the very words of God Himself! One of the greatest themes of God's providence throughout history is His presence with His people. This theme can be traced from His presence with Adam and Eve in the Garden, to the Tent of Meeting where He met Moses, to the

3. Nietzsche, *The Gay Science*, Section 125, tr. Walter Kaufmann

4. Thomas Jefferson, Benjamin Franklin, James Madison, Alexander Hamilton, and possibly even George Washington would be considered deists by most historians. Thomas Paine would also be included, who wrote *The Age of Reason* which popularized deism throughout the young nation.

Tabernacle where He met His people, to the more permanent structure of the Temple that God Himself designed as a meeting place for atonement in His presence.

But this is not merely an Old Testament phenomenon. We see the ultimate example of "God with us" in the coming of Jesus Christ, who is God, to earth as a human being.

"The Word (Jesus) became flesh and made His dwelling among us. We have seen His glory, the glory of the One and Only, who came from the Father, full of grace and truth." —John 1:14

Before Jesus' birth, the angel told Joseph,

"The virgin will be with child and will give birth to a son, and they will call Him Immanuel" — which means, "God with us." —Matthew 1:23

The presence of God was part of His divine plan for salvation that He promised ever since the fall of humanity into sin all the way back in Genesis 3. Contrary to the claims of this trailer for *Metro: Last Light*, not only did God stick around, but it is He who made certain His plan for salvation, even when we left Him!

"But God demonstrates His own love for us in this: While we were still sinners, Christ died for us." —Romans 5:8

The New Testament also describes how when Jesus returned to Heaven He would send a helper, the Holy Spirit to empower us and continue our salvation. God with us would now be God the Spirit dwelling in His people, the church! All of this leads to the eternal hope that Christians have when the Judgment Day arrives and we are taken to Heaven to be with God for all eternity, rejoicing and praising His name.

The fictional future of *Metro: Last Light* is one in which Judgment Day has already happened, but we know from God's Word that it is still ahead of us, and that because He is with us, our hope is secure.

> "Praise be to the God and Father of our Lord Jesus
> Christ! In His great mercy He has given us new birth
> into a living hope through the resurrection of Jesus
> Christ from the dead." — 1 Peter 1:3

Is there hope for humanity?

An understanding of God's overarching plan of salvation through history makes this question critical, but also easier to answer. We are not alone. Our hope does not rest in ourselves or in humanity to save us. This kind of hope is fleeting, as humans are prone to failure and corruption. Instead, God gives us a hope that is secure, not a wish or a want, but a confident hope based on the truth that, through Jesus, the salvation of believers is secure; the eternal victory is won.

> "But in your hearts set apart Christ as Lord. Always be
> prepared to give an answer to everyone who asks you
> to give the reason for the hope that you have. But do
> this with gentleness and respect." — 1 Peter 3:15

God's presence with us, His grace through Jesus Christ, is the most stunning, encouraging, and matchless promise made to us in God's Word. Far from being dead and gone, Jesus died to take the penalty of sin and rose again alive from the grave to conquer sin and death, so that we can experience eternal life through him and reconciliation to God, who is with us!

The Adventures of Darwin

System: Playstation 2
Rating: Everyone 10+
Year: 2007

The *Adventures of Darwin* is a strategy game released for Playstation 2 in 2007 in which you are responsible to develop a prehistoric village. The story begins with a monkey named

Darwin who has a terrible dream about a meteor that strikes earth and wipes out all life. Darwin lives in the village which is full of monkeys living in houses and drinking at bars. Darwin must convince his monkey brethren to go on a long adventure of Evolution to save the village.

On the journey you hunt other creatures and collect items to help you evolve. You evolve from a monkey to an ape-man to Cro-Magnon and so on, until you finally evolve into a human.

The Content:

At the end of the game you discover a portal to a far distant land. You meet a man with white robes and a crown of thorns hovering over his head and his name is God! So much for subtlety!

God: "I was wondering what that noise was… Just some monkeys I made from dirt. I have created many different life forms over the eons. This was to create my ideal world. But I keep messing up. Do you know why? When creatures live for a long time, they become greedy. 'I want more… more!' Then they quarrel and destroy.

You are the same, aren't you? Now you profit by eating another's meat. This isn't the world I wanted. You too emerged as a failed experiment. This planet has been on a cycle of creation and destruction. I have no choice but to give up on this planet and move to a new one.

This planet has been destroyed once, and has had to regenerate itself. Your adventure ends here too.

Hmm? You seem to have strong feelings about this. Do you want to keep this planet?

(Evil laugh)

Ha Ha! Well, you are greedy creatures. Will you destroy

me and survive as you did before?

Too bad, but I've already decided to destroy it. Just because you've slightly evolved, it doesn't mean you know yourself. Unlike the planet, you don't need to be reborn. You're not even worth dirt. You will disappear!"

A long battle ensues where God strikes you with his lightning bolts.

Eventually, you and your brothers manage to defeat God prompting the following speech:

"How dreadful… You seem to have a greater attachment to life than I. Fair enough, I'll give you this planet. Do with it as you like. I wonder what kind of future will befall us.

Allow me to give you one final offering. How you will use it is up to you… In tens of thousands of years, I will visit this planet again. At that time, I look forward to seeing how you are all faring."

God then disappears, but leaves a present: a pistol. Twenty thousand years later, God reappears to find nothing but dead bodies and gravestones. In an I-told-you-so manner, God demeans his own creation as a mistake with these final thoughts:

"You foolish monkeys. It's quite clear that the 'pistol' I sent you has worsened your greed. It's proof that you cannot go against who you are. In the next life I'll try not to make the same mistake."

The Challenge:
Are we monkeys made from dirt? Does God make mistakes?
This is a decidedly non-biblical representation of God, not

dissimilar to the "set-it-and-forget-it" view of deism. Here God created a world, but left it to its own devices after realizing that it was a mistake. It is a world for which he could care less and ultimately decides to destroy as he continues his trial and error process to create a world that is good. This is also a direct challenge to the creation as told to us in Genesis, the first book of the Bible. The whole story is built on the evolution of humanity from monkeys, which goes against the biblical record.

The Answers:
Are we just monkeys made from dirt?

Sometimes the most dangerous challenges are the ones that carry a slice of truth but twist or add to it. However, this one is pretty easy to spot. Was the first man, Adam, made from dirt? Yes. But are we just monkeys? No, not at all!

In the record of creation, the Bible says,

> *"The Lord God formed the man from the dust of the ground, and breathed into his nostrils the breath of life, and man became a living being." —Genesis 2:7*

We are different and separate from animals, like monkeys, because we are created in God's image.

> *"So God created man in His own image, in the image of God He created him; male and female He created them." —Genesis 1:27*

God gave us a special task to "fill the earth and subdue it"[5] and every human since then can trace their family line back to Adam and Eve, not through evolution through monkeys or any other creature.

Does God make mistakes?

This challenge is an interesting one because some atheists and skeptics challenge the concept of God's omnipotence or

---

5.   Genesis 1:28

omnibenevolence by pointing to the evil that exists in a world created by a good God. Yet, in this same passage in Genesis, we see that God did not consider His creation a mistake despite the actions of those who sinned against Him, bringing evil into the world!

> *"God saw all that He had made, and it was very good. And there was evening, and there was morning – the sixth day. Thus the heavens and the earth were completed in all their vast array." —Genesis 1:31–2:1*

Even after the deceit of the snake and the sinful fall of man, God did not look at His creation or us as a mistake to be destroyed. Instead, He loves us and wants to redeem us. From the very moment of the fall, we see that God had a plan to redeem creation and offer us salvation from the brokenness that entered the world through people.

> *"For if, by the trespass of the one man, death reigned through that one man, how much more will those who receive God's abundant provision of grace and of the gift of righteousness reign in life through the one man, Jesus Christ." —Romans 5:17*

Far from abandoning us to our sin, we see a God who loves us enough to bear with us for a time so that His plan of salvation can be worked out.

> *"As for God, His way is perfect; the word of the Lord is proven; He is a shield to all those that trust in Him." —Psalm 18:30*

Dragon Quest IX

System: Nintendo DS
Rating: E10+
Year: 2010

Dragon Quest IX is an entry into one of the most popular RPG series in gaming history, especially in Japan where it originated. The highly touted series has also found a diehard following in English speaking territories. A number of the games have vague depictions of higher powers like goddesses or demon kings, but the series also has several direct representations of God.

One such example is when "God" appears as a secret boss in *Dragon Quest VII* on the Playstation (soon to be re-released for Nintendo 3DS), but a more substantial example is right here in *Dragon Quest IX*. In the game, you play as a Celestrian (read: Angel) who has fallen from the heavens to the earth and must aid mortals in restoring their faith in the Celestrians.

The Content:

Toward the end of the game you witness this fascinating conversation between "Almighty" creator of everything, Zenus, and his daughter Celestria.

"Zenus: …Yea, the mortals are not fit to inhabit my Kingdom. They are an aberration. From dust they came, and to dust I shall return them.

Celestria: I beg of you! Stay your hand!

Zenus: Wherefore do you defy me? What cause have you to give them succor?

Celestria: Father, I—I have faith in the mortals. You cannot—you must not—lay waste to their realm… I beg of thee…

Zenus: You dare question my will? You dare obstruct my purpose?

(Celestria turns into a tree)

Zenus: Celestria! What is this insolence!?

Celestria: If it be the only way to save mortalkind, I shall take on this form. I shall become Yggdrasil, the World Tree. My body shall be returned only when the good that lies within mortal hearts is proven... There is purity in the mortal soul... There is good... I will prove this to you, though it cost me my freedom...

Zenus: Impetuous child! You know not what foolishness you contemplate, Celestria! If no such proof should present itself, you will be cursed to eternal slumber! My child... What have you done?

...So be it. Your rashness has stayed my hand. The mortals shall live. Let there be beings to serve your purpose. Let these beings stand ever-vigilant over mortalkind, awaiting proof of the purity within...

But know this, Celestria: the day of your awakening may never come...

The Challenge:
Does God hate us because of our failures?
While Zenus seems to be something of an amalgamation of various religions, there are no doubt very significant parallels to Christianity. Celestria, though a daughter, represents the only child whose purpose is to save humanity from the impending wrath of God. She sacrifices her life (turning into a tree) much like Jesus was God's only Son who sacrificed His life (on a tree) to take on the sins of the world and offer us eternal life. In the game, the Yggdrasil tree Celestria turns into is a "tree of life," the leaves of which can resurrect dead characters.

However, where God the Father and Jesus the Son have the same purpose for salvation, Zenus and Celestria are at odds with each other. It paints a common picture in video games where God hates humanity because of their failures and wants to give up on them before some hero comes along and either changes his mind or kills him.

Is any of this biblically accurate? Does God hate us because of our failures?

The Answers:

In *Dragon Quest IX*, God says that there are no mortals who are deserving of entering his kingdom. This is actually true, as Paul, quoting Isaiah, tells us,

> *"As it is written, There is no one righteous,*
> *not even one."* —Romans 3:10

Yet he goes on in this same passage to describe how we are made righteous with a righteousness that comes from God through faith in Jesus Christ, even though we are all sinners.[6] Paul also writes,

> *"Here is a trustworthy saying that deserves full accep-*
> *tance: Christ Jesus came into the world to save sin-*
> *ners—of whom I am the worst. But for that very reason*
> *I was shown mercy so that in me, the worst of sinners,*
> *Christ Jesus might display His unlimited patience as*
> *an example for those who would believe on Him and*
> *receive eternal life."* —1 Timothy 1:15–16

Many of us, knowing our own failures, can sympathize with Paul's sense of his own sinfulness. Paul was a man who not only doubted Jesus, but was actively putting His followers to death before having his own conversion experience. Does he say that God hates him? No. He describes Jesus' unending patience and love even for the chief of sinners who turns to faith in Christ.

> *"But God demonstrates His own love for us in this:*

---

6.   Romans 3:22-23

While we were still sinners, Christ died for us."
—Romans 5:8

El Shaddai: Ascension of the Metatron

System: Playstation 3, Xbox 360
Rating: Teens
Year: 2011
Publisher: UTV Ignition Entertainment
Developer: Ignition Tokyo

El Shaddai: Ascension of the Metatron follows a character named Enoch, a priest seeking seven fallen angels to prevent a great flood from destroying mankind. He is helped in his quest by Lucifel (Lucifer) and four Arch Angels.

From this simple description you can already see a plethora of biblical connections. El Shaddai is actually one of the names of God found in the Old Testament, used in Exodus and the book of Job. It is usually translated "God Almighty." There are the references to Angels, Lucifer (discussed in Chapter 5) and even Enoch who was a real man in the Bible and whose story is recorded in Genesis 5:22–29 and mentioned in Hebrews 11:5. He is known for the fact that he did not die, but was taken to heaven without experiencing physical death. He was also an ancestor of Noah, another interesting connection as the game makes mention of preventing a destructive flood.

The Content:

At one point in the game your character, Enoch, travels to "the Tower." The game explains the significance of this location.

"The Tower… The Fallen Angels left Heaven, hiding themselves from God's eyes. People flocked to the false world they created, and were covered by a veil.

The people flourished and reveled in civilization. They

worshipped the Fallen Angels, and forgot God.

Our prayers can no longer be heard by God."

Throughout the game, Lucifel talks to God on the phone. The devil is God's right hand man and watches over Enoch. In one scene there is a character named "Sin" who is dying. Lucifel stands over the dying man.

Sin: Thank you… Thank you for hearing my story. You… Are you… God…? So I… shall go to Heaven…"

(Sin dies. Lucifel picks up his cell phone to call God.) Lucifel: "Yeah… uh huh… I was mistaken for you again… hahahahaha."

God and Lucifel have a good laugh about how they always get mistaken for each other.

The Challenge:
Does God hear our prayers?
This game borrows from the Bible for plot details, treating it as just another interesting mythology to be mined for story ideas. This means that many of the concepts and references in the game bear almost no resemblance to their scriptural counterparts. It stands as another example of watering down the message of the Bible to nothing more than a collection of myths. This is a dangerous trend in gaming and broader culture. One point beyond this that we will take a moment to address is the statement that "our prayers can no longer be heard by God."

The Answer:
There are many instances in the Bible where God demonstrates that He hears and answers prayers in the lives of individuals. He calls us to a personal relationship where we "cast

all your anxiety upon Him because He cares for you."[7] Likewise, we are assured that our prayers are heard by God when they are prayers made in faith and in line with His will for our lives.

> *"This is the confidence which we have before Him,*
> *that, if we ask anything according to His will, He hears*
> *us. And if we know that He hears us in whatever we*
> *ask, we know that we have the requests which we*
> *have asked from Him." — 1 John 5:14–15*

---

7. 1 Peter 5:7

Conversation Questions

- What comes to mind when you think of God? How would you describe Him?

- Check out these passages to get some ideas about a few of the attributes of God: 1 John 4:16; Matthew 19:26; Romans 1:17; Exodus 20:5–6; Isaiah 6:3; Romans 11:22.

- What does it mean that God is omnipotent, omnipresent, and omnibenevolent? Why is this important?

- In light of who God is why should we trust His plan for us if we follow Him obediently?

- How can we talk to God? Can He hear us? Try a simple prayer to God right now thanking Him for His goodness and sovereignty.

- Where do we find hope? How would you explain the source of hope? Who is one person with whom you can share that hope?

Online Gaming Tips

MANY OF THE games available today include options to play online. They pit players against other players anywhere in the world. This adds a level of excitement to the experience and connects gamers worldwide, but it also adds a great deal of risk. This chapter is especially directed at parents, as gamers may already be aware of some of these tips and tricks, but it will be valuable as a reminder for gamers as well to always be vigilant, careful, and godly when playing or doing anything online. Before playing online yourself or allowing your children to play online games, take some time to understand the risks of online gaming.

What to know before you go online

Children might download the bad with the good:

Games are often downloaded from links received in emails, instant messages, or text messages. Some of these might link to less-than-reputable sites. Your child might download what appears to be a good game, but the download might also contain offensive content, spam, or malware.

Children might be tricked into providing personal information:

Some of these "free" games require extensive profiles,

which ask for personal information. Once the game distributor has this information, they could illegally sell it for personal gain without consideration of how it will be used. The information could also be given away or used with malicious intent. Remember that the information provided for a profile will likely include the gamer's age.

Children might be bullied or exposed to bad language:

Some gamers play simply to harass and taunt other players. They might use inappropriate or foul language, or they might bully other players by cheating or through intimidation.

Children might make friends with the wrong people:

There are predators out there that will pretend to be children and try to earn the trust of under-age gamers. They might share tips on how to win, giving gifts like points, or offer to correspond via email or phone. Their intent is never good. They might be trying to run a scam or to arrange to meet in person.

How to create the right environment for online play

If, after evaluating the risks, you decide to allow your child to engage in online gaming, then there are some important things to remember.

1. Train your children how to play online games responsibly. Point out to them the dangers and what they should watch for. Remind them to report anything suspicious to you (not just tell their friends).

2. Engage with your children while they play online. Observe the games and the emotions involved with this activity. Make sure both are healthy and God-honoring.

3. Be aware of how your children use the internet—not just gaming, but everywhere they go on the worldwide web. It really is a type of "web" and it can capture their attention and their affection.

4. Set limits and boundaries. Set boundaries on where they can go, but also set restrictions on how much time is devoted to gaming. If they spend all their time gaming, they aren't doing other important things like reading God's Word and growing spiritually. Moderation is key to healthy gaming.

5. Teach your children to keep personal information a secret. Children should never give any personal information to any website or person online, especially without consent of a parent.

6. Children must watch their own conduct online. Remind them that they are children of the King and so they are His ambassadors. They should always represent Him well, in what they say, what they think and what they do.

Be discerning:

"Teach me knowledge and good judgment, for I believe in your commands." —Psalm 119:66

Discipline your children:

"Listen, my son, to your father's instruction and do not forsake your mother's teaching." —Proverbs 1:8

Disciple your children:

"Train a child in the way he should go, and when he is old he will not turn from it." —Proverbs 22:6

And always remember:

"The highway of the upright avoids evil; he who guards his way guards his life." —Proverbs 16:17

Parents, did you know?

If you own a video game console, you can control things like:

Which games can be played.

Which movies and TV shows can be watched.

How long each family member can use the console.

Whether or not someone can access the internet.

Levels of online safety and privacy settings for child accounts.
Resources for Parental Controls

Xbox 360

http://support.xbox.com/en-US/billing-and-subscriptions/
parental-controls/xbox-live-parental-control

Nintendo Wii

http://www.nintendo.com/consumer/systems/wii/en_na/
ht_settings.jsp

Playstation 3

http://manuals.playstation.net/document/en/ps3/current/
basicoperations/parentallock.html

Know it!
Live it!
Share it!

STILL THINK "IT'S just a game?" By now, we hope you are willing to reconsider, as we have seen many examples of games and developers that approach Christianity from many different perspectives. Some have merely borrowed names or settings for story ideas, treating Christianity as an interesting mythology. Others intentionally explore the benefits and consequences of religion without tipping the hand of the developer's own opinion. And some demonstrate downright contempt for the Christian faith and the people who believe it.

It is important to be equipped to answer the challenges the games bring to the Bible. It is a stark reminder that no area of life, even the seemingly innocuous area of entertainment, is immune from the enemy's attacks. In fact, in describing the signs that the end times are near, Jesus warns his disciples,

"All men will hate you because of me." —Luke 21:17

And again,

"If you belonged to the world, it would love you as its own. As it is, you do not belong to the world, but

*I have chosen you out of the world. That is why the
world hates you." —John 15:19*

Do Jesus' strong words describe the opposition that *might*
come when we live for Him? No, He warns us against what *will*
happen! These are strong words, but notice also what is absent: He does not call us to hate the world in return. Rather, this
warning comes on the heels of a passage in which Jesus describes how we will bear fruit for the gospel by remaining in Him.

So what should we do? How do we prepare to answer the
challenges, both direct and indirect, that we will face as we live
in a lost world, trying to reach lost people with His truth?

We set ourselves a challenge at the beginning of the book to
learn how to think critically by applying God's truth to the games
around us by using a simple strategy: Know it. Live it. Share it.
Now we bring it all together as this simple strategy for taking
what we've learned back to these or other games. We now
have the ability to recognize and respond to challenges.

We must Know It! Live It! and Share It!

Know It!

Hopefully this book has given you some knowledge on how
the video game industry is challenging God's Word. We have to
know what the secular worldview is, but more importantly we
need to know what the Bible teaches.

"Test everything. Hold on to the good."
— 1 Thessalonians 5:21

Christians need to strive to be like the Bereans, as described
in Acts,

*"Now the Bereans were of more noble character than
the Thessalonians, for they received the message with
great eagerness and examined the Scriptures every
day to see if what Paul said was true." —Acts 17:11*

The Bereans were commended for testing even the words of the Apostle Paul against the Scriptures. We base everything on His truth, testing every game, even this very book, with His revealed truth in the Bible.

It takes a little practice, but if you slow down enough to recognize the spiritual content in video games, it becomes second nature to run everything through the filter of God's Word. In some sense, the examples here are like case studies giving a blue print of how to do just that: study God's Word and apply it to games. When we do this, our knowledge becomes more than just facts and details, it becomes a powerful tool to live the truth and share the truth.

Live It!

Once we know what Scripture says, we need to do our best, through the power of the Holy Spirit, to live as the Bible guides us. It can be difficult knowing where to draw the line on which games we play or allow our children to play. We have avoided direct statements of "play" or "don't play" throughout this book for that very reason. It is more important for you to learn to apply Scripture in every situation, not just these specific games. The time taken to learn that skill is much more valuable than avoiding the challenges via a wholesale game dump!

All video games are not evil, but it is very important that we know to what we are exposing ourselves and our children.

> *"Finally, brethren, whatsoever things are true, whatsoever things are honest, whatsoever things are just, whatsoever things are pure, whatsoever things are lovely, whatsoever things are of good report; if there be any virtue, and if there be any praise, think on these things."* —Philippians 4:8 NKJV

There are video games being produced today that are not good, or even neutral—they are sinful. The Bible warns us not to love the things of the world.

> *"Do not love the world, or anything in the world. If any-one loves the world, the love of the Father is not in him."* —1 John 2:15

It is extremely difficult to take something we enjoy so much, like video games, and cast them aside for the sake of Christ. Not every game must be avoided, but we should be willing to dump any game if we are more attached to the game than to Christ. A simple test is to pray about the game. If you don't want to check in with God about a game, that's a red flag.

It takes a bold person to look in the mirror, or at our game collection, and willingly make a significant change about what we put into our minds. Approach the decision prayerfully, willing to cast aside even your favorite game, if you test it and it is not good.

Share It!

In researching for this book, we have had many conversations with one another and many more with parents. Whenever we talk to parents about the content of the games their children play, they are almost always completely clueless about the anti-Christian worldviews being touted in video games already in the home. It is subtle, but it is a full-out attack.

With a culture that is extremely confident of its rejection of biblical truth and its attack on God's truth, we need to be just as confident with a message of hope! We need to be ready to provide answers.

> *"But in your hearts set apart Christ as Lord. Always be prepared to give an answer to everyone who asks you to give the reason for the hope that you have. But do this with gentleness and respect."* —1 Peter 3:15

The world can be a very dark place, but the gospel of Jesus

Christ is light in a dark world. We must rely on the Word of God to be our authority, and we must be ready to share that good news with others! Many spiritual conversations and opportunities for the gospel are born out of our everyday experience, so keep your eyes open for those moments in games where spiritual truth is challenged and let the Holy Spirit guide your spiritual conversations as you introduce people to the only true source of hope, Jesus Christ!

Starting Points for Parents

Understand the ESRB (or PEGI) Ratings

The ratings systems are not perfect. They don't focus on the spiritual content at all, which is a big part of why books and conversations like this are necessary. With that said, it is still a very helpful tool for parents and gamers to understand other elements of games like violence, sexuality, etc. (For more on individual ratings, visit www.esrb.org for U.S. ratings or www.pegi.info for European ratings.)

Talk with your children

It is important to know that the world has an agenda and a message. Don't fall into the trap of thinking it's just a game! We must be in God's Word and talking about God's Word to know the real truth! It can be intimidating to talk to our children about video games if we don't know much about them ourselves, so use this book and especially the Conversation Questions as a guide to get the discussion going. Don't look for an "easy" way out like banning all video games, but take the time to have open and challenging discussions, teaching your children to think critically for themselves!

Get involved

Carl once visited a church in the Midwest that had a very strong youth program. Inside the church they had a video game room, which the children loved. However, the leader had very strict rules. He required that any game that the children would play had to first be played by an assigned adult leader, from beginning to end! That's no easy task. But because of this, they knew exactly what their children were playing. Find creative ways to play the game yourself, play together with your child, or even just keep the games in a "public" area of the house. This helps you to know what's in the game, and makes you more available for timely spiritual conversations with your gamer.

Know your options

Your children may ask you to buy them a game, but it may contain content with which you don't feel comfortable. Just because their friends are playing the game, doesn't mean it's the only fun game. There are worse things than not being able to play the latest Triple A title. Don't feel comfortable with your child playing the T rated racing game *Test Drive Unlimited 2*? Recommend another excellent racing game, *Gran Turismo 5*, which is rated E. It takes a little effort, but working together to find game alternatives can be a great bonding experience.

Starting Points for Gamers

Be honest with your parents!

We're now writing to the young gamers out there now. We know there are some video games that you want to play, but your parents don't approve. Still, be honest with your parents about the content of the games.

Call of Duty 4: Modern Warfare is one of the most popular games of all-time. Children will tell their parents, "I play it because I want to support our troops!" or "It's impossible to kill anyone, they just come back to life in multi-player." But that isn't the full truth. The game was rated M because of Blood and Gore, Drug References, Intense Violence, and Strong Language.

Being honest with your parents builds a lot of trust that will go a long way. You don't have to wait on your parents! You can get the spiritual conversations started. Help them understand gaming, and work together to understand God's Word!

Read the Bible

The straight-up truth is that the world has a secular worldview that doesn't line up with Scripture. How many hours do you play video games in a day? How many hours do your read the Bible? The Bible is the only place you will find the Biblical Worldview, so you can discern fact from fiction.

We don't ask that to make you feel guilty. Many Christians struggle to find time for daily Bible intake, but it is one of the most important, most helpful, and honestly, most exciting things you will ever do! Jesus wants to give you an amazing new life when you are ready to follow Him in all things on a daily basis.

If you don't feel comfortable playing a game, DON'T!

Carl remembers when *Grand Theft Auto 3* first came out and he went to a friend's house to play it. His friend thought it was hilarious and cool that you could pick up prostitutes, carjack vehicles, and kill police officers. Carl didn't find it very funny. Carl walked out of his friend's house and went home. Yes, it was embarrassing, but it was also bold. It is far more important to be faithful to God than to our friends. That uncomfortable feeling is often the Holy Spirit warning you that you are about to get into something that is not pleasing to God and will leave damage behind. Don't ignore the Holy Spirit when He uses your conscience to warn you! In a similar experience, though a different game, a friend came up to Carl after the fact and thanked him that someone finally walked out of something that wasn't pleasing God. It may be embarrassing, but it can have big-time impact on you and the person you encouraged.

Do your research

There are some games in this book that we played for personal enjoyment, not because we wanted to do research (though we kept our notes close as you never know when a spiritual scene will show up!). We need to be aware of what we are playing and what is in each game. Because so many people are unaware of the spiritual content in games, it is often difficult to know beforehand what you might encounter. At the same time, there is so much information online that you have a lot of ways to do some pre-purchase digging. If you get the game home and encounter something you didn't expect, don't just let it pass by. Test it against the Bible! Hold on to the good, and be willing to dump the bad.

Conclusion

Games can open the door to many opportunities to share the gospel with our children and other gamers because they include so many religious themes and references! Imagine having the confidence to follow the Holy Spirit's leading into a conversation where instead of saying "I think games are bad," you could instead say, "Let me show you who the Bible tells us God really is!"

Gamers, we must know God's Word, live God's Word, and share God's Word! We pray that Christ will move through this culture, draw people to Himself, and the kingdom will expand because of parents and gamers who know:

It's NOT just a game!

Index of Games

Scripture Index

General Index

About the Authors

Carl Kerby Jr. founded *"It's Not Just a Game"* ministries with Drew Thorwall and is a high impact nationwide speaker and guest on radio shows with Moody and Focus on the Family. He has a B.A. in Media Studies and a passion for teaching parents and reaching gamers. He and his wife, Tish, are blessed with two children: Trey and Naomi.

Carl's Gamer Profile: "I own a ton of classic gaming systems, even less successful gems like Nintendo's Virtual Boy. The collection is a great way to relax and do research at the same time! I especially love the old-school games and finding new challenges to master from some of the more difficult ones (still working on Silver Surfer for NES...)"

Drew Thorwall is a pastor, writer, husband, and father. He received his Master's of Divinity from Trinity Evangelical Divinity School in Deerfield, IL. He has a passion for using games to start spiritual conversations with gamers. He and his wife, Melissa, are blessed with four children: Belle, Axel, Obed, and Simeon.

Drew's Gamer Profile: "Super Nintendo was the first system I owned and the golden age of games, especially for RPG's. Lufia II, Final Fantasy III (actually VI) and Earthbound were some of my favorites. I love classic games like Super Metroid, and recent games like Portal 2. Game cred comes from the fact that I can take on any challenger with Luigi in Super Smash Bros."

Additional Resources
Available through www.injagame.com

It's Not Just a Game – Season 1 (DVD)
This one is for the parents. This companion DVD digs into several of the games from the book, and many more! Included are topics such as Suicide in Videogames and extra features only available on the DVD.

Apologaming – Season 1 (DVD)
This one is for the gamers. Video series and study guide for Small Group or family use addressing real answers to many of the difficult questions skeptics ask about the Bible.

Biblically Handling Technology and Social Media
Tips for teens and parents on technology and social media (cell phones, video games, etc.) Contributions from Carl Kerby Jr. and Drew Thorwall.

Online
Videos, game reviews, articles and more!

Find us on Youtube:
Search for "injagame" and Subscribe!

"Like us" on Facebook
www.facebook.com/videogameministry